Bouncing Eggs

OTHER BOOKS BY WILLIAM R. WELLNITZ:

Homemade Slime & Rubber Bones! Awesome Science Activities

Science Magic for Kids: 68 Simple & Safe Activities

Science in Your Backyard

Be a Kid Physicist

Bouncing Eggs

Amazing Science Activities You Can Do at Home

William R. Wellnitz

McGraw-Hill

New York San Francisco Washington, D.C. Auckland Bogotá
Caracas Lisbon London Madrid Mexico City Milan
Montreal New Delhi San Juan Singapore
Sydney Tokyo Toronto

McGraw-Hill

A Division of The McGraw·Hill Companies

1 2 3 4 5 6 7 8 9 0   DOC/DOC   9 0 9 8 7 6 5 4 3 2 1 0 9

ISBN 0-07-134383-0

The sponsoring editor for this book was Griffin Hansbury, the editing supervisor was Patricia V. Amoroso, and the production supervisor was Clare B. Stanley. It was set in Tykewriter by PJ Smith.

Printed and bound by R.R. Donnelley & Sons Company

The experiments and activities in this book should be performed with care and according to the instructions provided. An adult should supervise young readers who undertake these experiments. The publisher and author accept no responsibility for any damage caused or sustained while performing any of the activities or experiments in this book.

 This book is printed on recycled, acid-free paper containing a minimum of 50% recycled de-inked paper.

Contents

NOTES TO CHILDREN

I wrote this book for you to have fun with science. Your kitchen or yard can become your own science laboratory. You don't need fancy equipment. Almost everything you need should be found in your home.

Many of the experiments may surprise you. They may seem like magic, and you can amaze your friends with tricks. But the experiments are not magic. They all are based on the rules of science.

Look through the book and find one or two experiments you find interesting. Each experiment tells at the start what happens. Gather all the materials you will need for the experiment. Keep the materials in one place.

Become familiar with the safety warnings at the tops of many experiments. They provide you with all the safety precautions you should practice. Pay special attention to whether you should have an adult present. Always keep safety in mind when doing any experiment. You should probably have an adult with you when you do any of the experiments.

Now read the procedure, but do not read the explanation until you have done the experiment. You are now ready to do the experiment. Follow the directions exactly as they are written. Look at the pictures to see if you have set up things correctly.

Use all of your senses as you observe what happens. If you must write something down, do it as soon as you make the measurement. Your memory is often not as good as it seems. Try to explain what happened and why. You might want to repeat the experiment one or two more times. Now look at the explanation to see if you figured it out. Try to talk about the experiment with an adult.

After you have done the experiment, try doing the things listed in Other Things to Try, or try changing some of the materials and experiment on your own. Be curious! Have fun! Always be safe!

If you have questions or did some new and interesting things, or would just like to comment on the book or chat with me, please write to me:

Dr. Bill Wellnitz
Biology Department
Augusta State University
Augusta, Georgia 30904

Some of the experiments in this book were sent to me by kids who had used some of my other books!

If you have a computer, you can also e-mail me at wwellnit@aug.edu. Speaking of computers, I have found some really neat web sites that have lots of cool stuff about science, including some more experiments you can do.

www.exploratorium.edu. This is the site for a great science museum in San Francisco.

www.msichicago.org. The Museum of Science and Industry in Chicago.

www.4kids.org. A site that has lots of information and many other exciting places to visit.

NOTES TO ADULTS

This book had its origin with my children, all of whom are now grown but not too old to still enjoy many of the things in this book. Many times when they had friends over, rather than making cookies, we would do science experiments in the kitchen. Our kitchen became a wonderful laboratory, and soon the number of children wanting to do kitchen science exceeded the space of our kitchen. By 1989, the demand for science experiments and experience grew into three different week-end continuing education science classes for children at Augusta State University. Since that initial offering, over 1200 students have participated in "Wizard Wellnitz", and two local television stations have recently begun airing these science clips.

The intent of this book is threefold:

1. to expose children to principles and procedures of science

2. to show children that science is and can be fun

3. to stimulate thinking and creativity.

By showing young children that science is fun, I hope to encourage them to maintain an interest in and an appreciation for science.

Understanding scientific concepts requires active participation, but it is not necessary to use sophisticated equipment. Stimulating creative thinking often involves exposure to a discrepant, or surprising, event. Convincing children that science is fun demands that they be allowed to play and experiment on their own.

Consequently, the simple, safe experiments in this book 1) use items that are readily available in the home, 2) often appear as magic tricks, and 3) are open-ended. All experiments have been kid-tested many times, and most require less than 30 minutes to complete.

Although most experiments can be done by children alone, you probably want to become involved, but only as a guide. Some experiments demand your assistance and should not be done by children alone. These experiments require the use of a stove, flames, or electricity; such experiments are clearly indicated at the start of each experiment. Help them find the materials, but let them do the experiment themselves. Discuss the results with them and encourage them to think of explanations and other uses of the process involved.

Two important aspects of science are observation and measurement. Encourage your children to use all their senses, to measure accurately, and to record their observations.

Many of the experiments are intentionally open-ended. Children are naturally curious and will want to vary the procedure or try different materials. Don't become alarmed if they do this; just make certain they do the experiment as written on their first attempt. Many a great discovery has come from someone modifying an existing procedure.

The experiments in this book provide a solid background in scientific principles and methodology, and the techniques can easily be applied to other situations. Many of the experiments, especially those items listed in Other Things to Try, could easily become science-fair projects, but my intent is not to provide a listing of science-fair projects. If your child does a science-fair project, be sure that he or she actually does the work.

Finally, you may enjoy many of the experiments; and if you have a fear of science, you too may discover that science can be fun. You may even want to set up some of the demos when you have company. I welcome your comments, both positive and negative; my address appears in Notes to Children.

Acknowledgments

Thanks to Judith Terrill-Breuer for help with the initial stages of the book; Griffin Hansbury, Pattie Amoroso, and Paula Jo Smith for layout and numerous editorial activities; Jessica Jernigan for the drawings; and my family for their support.

Unit 1
Rubbery and Gooey Things

This section contains experiments that produce items that seem rubbery or gooey. Some of the changes result from dissolving or breaking chemical structures; other changes result from hooking different things together.

Soap bubbles are some of the neatest things to play with. This section also contains lots of fun things you can do with soap bubbles. To do many of the experiments, you will need to make a good soap bubble mix. Most dish detergents will work, but *Joy* and *Dawn* brands work best. You may want to have an adult help you measure to make the mix.

SUPER SOAP MIX:

✔ 1 part dish detergent (for example, 3-4 teaspoons, or 25 mL)

✔ 12 parts water (for example, 1 1/2 cups, or about 300 mL)

Gently mix the detergent and water. Try not to make too many bubbles. You want the film, not lots of small bubbles. Mixtures with many bubbles will not make big bubbles. Let this mixture sit for a few minutes before you use it.

Sometimes you may have to use only 10 parts of water or maybe 15 parts. As the mixture begins to be used up, add more water, not more detergent. You can make the bubbles stronger by adding 2-3 teaspoons (5-20 mL) of glycerin to the bubble mix.

#1

The Bouncing Egg

What you need
- ✔ egg
- ✔ jar with lid big enough to hold the egg
- ✔ vinegar
- ✔ sauce pan
- ✔ stove

TIME REQUIRED
5-10 minutes each day over a week; then 10 minutes

WHAT TO DO

1. Fill the jar with vinegar.

2. Place egg in a jar and cover the jar.

3. Change the vinegar every couple of days and turn the egg each time so that all of the shell is exposed to the vinegar.

4. After a few days, remove the egg from the vinegar. Notice that the shell of the egg is gone.

5. Hold the egg a few inches or centimeters above the countertop or sink.

6. Drop the egg. If you drop the egg from too high above the counter, the egg will still break.

7. Watch what happens to the egg.

WHAT'S HAPPENING AND WHY:

Certain minerals in the egg shell make it hard. The vinegar removes these minerals, and the shell dissolves. At this point, the egg is more like a ball than an egg. The liquid inside the egg behaves like air inside a ball.

OTHER THINGS TO TRY:

Have an adult boil the egg before soaking it in the vinegar. Does the shell still disappear? To model what is happening to the shell, place a small piece of chalk in vinegar and observe the chalk every day.

DISCOVERY

Eggs usually break when they are dropped. In this experiment, you will make an egg that bounces, not one that cracks.

3

#2 Blowing Giant Soap Bubbles

What you need

- ✔ soap bubble mix (see introduction to Unit 1)
- ✔ plastic soft-drink bottle
- ✔ scissors
- ✔ shallow pan or cookie sheet

TIME REQUIRED

about 5 minutes to make the horn; at least 10 minutes to play with bubbles

WHAT TO DO

1. Have an adult help you cut the soft-drink bottle into the shape shown at left.

2. Place the soap bubble mix in the pan or cookie sheet.

3. Place your horn into the mix, and then remove it from the mix.

4. Gently blow into the horn to make a giant bubble.

5. To release the bubble into the air, turn the horn and pull it upward.

WHAT'S HAPPENING AND WHY:

 As you blow into the horn, your breath gets trapped in the film of soap. The air pushes on the film and makes a bubble. This simple device allows you to reuse something you usually throw out.

OTHER THINGS TO TRY:

Try using other things such as straws to blow bubbles. You can make the bubbles move in different directions by moving your hand on the side of the bubble. Moving air pushes less than nonmoving air, so if the bubble is sinking, move your hand above the bubble.

To make giant bubbles with string, cut a long piece of thick string and tie it together. After you dip the string into the bubble mix, spread the string out with your fingers and either blow into the soap or pull the string through the air.

Or, dip the string into the mix, and pull the spread string out of the mix. This will create a ghost or a long tube bubble that you can try to cover a friend with.

DISCOVERY
Make a "horn" from objects that you normally throw out. Use this "horn" to blow giant soap bubbles.

Bubbles Inside of Bubbles

What you need

✔ soap bubble mix (see introduction to Unit 1)

✔ many pipe cleaners or small pieces of thin wire

✔ deep pan such as a bread loaf pan

TIME REQUIRED

5 minutes to make the mix; 5-10 minutes to make the shape; 10 or more minutes to play

WHAT TO DO

1. Bend the pipe cleaners or wire and hook them together to form a cube.

2. Pour the soap mix into the deep pan. The mix should be deep enough to cover the cube you just made.

3. Hold one corner of the cube and dip the entire cube into the mix.

4. Remove the cube from the soap and hold it in the air for 20-30 seconds. At first, the soap will form walls on the cube, then suddenly a small soap cube will appear in the middle of the cube's frame.

5. After you see the small cube, move the pipe cleaner through the air to release the bubble. What shape bubble is released?

WHAT'S HAPPENING AND WHY:

 As the cube is exposed to the air, some of the water evaporates and leaves the mix. The soap film is pulled toward the center of the cube, but it is still attached to the pipe cleaner. When the edges of the film meet, they form a shape identical to the original frame.

Bubbles formed from any shape will always make a sphere in the air. Without walls to support the soap, it falls into a shape that needs almost no support, a sphere.

OTHER THINGS TO TRY:

TRY MAKING many different three-dimensional shapes out of pipe cleaners to see what happens.

TRY USING a variety of different shaped objects such as plastic rings from soft drinks, plastic strawberry containers, and even your hand to make different kinds of bubbles.

Once the bubble has formed, **TRY GENTLY** blowing into it with a straw. If you are lucky and careful, you will blow a bubble inside of another bubble.

BUBBLE, Heal Thyself!

What you need

- ✔ soap mix (see introduction to Unit 1)
- ✔ pipe cleaners or thick string
- ✔ shallow pan or cookie sheet
- ✔ pencil or straw (optional)

TIME REQUIRED

 about 5 minutes to make the mix; 5-15 minutes to play

WHAT TO DO

1. Use the pipe cleaners or heavy string to make a circle about 4-6 inches (10-15 cm) in diameter.

2. Fill the shallow pan with the soap mix.

3. Dip the circle into the mix. Remove the shape from the mix. You should see the film attached to the pipe cleaner. If you do not see the film, dip the pipe cleaner again.

4. Slowly push your wet finger or pencil through the film and then remove it.

5. Repeat step 4 as often as you can.

6. Release the bubble into the air when you are finished.

WHAT'S HAPPENING AND WHY:

The chemicals in the soap mix are attracted to each other, and also to your wet finger or pencil. When you remove your finger or pencil, the chemicals rush to get back together, and the hole in the bubble is patched.

DISCOVERY
See what happens when you stick a pencil in a bubble!

OTHER THINGS TO TRY:

Determine how many times you can punch a hole in the bubble and still keep the bubble intact. Try punching more than one hole at a time. What is the most number of holes you can punch at one time and not have the bubble break?

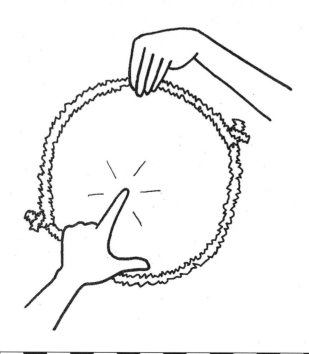

#5

The Floppy Bone

 ## TIME REQUIRED
1-2 weeks after initial set up

What you need
- ✔ chicken leg or wing bone
- ✔ tall glass or jar
- ✔ 2 or 3 bottles of vinegar

WHAT TO DO

1. Remove as much meat as possible from the bone. Place the bone in the jar.

2. Pour the vinegar into the jar until the bone is completely covered.

3. Change the vinegar in the jar every 3 or 4 days. Pour the old vinegar down the sink and rinse the sink with water.

4. After 1-2 weeks, remove the bone from the jar. It will now be very floppy, not stiff.

WHAT'S HAPPENING AND WHY:

 A chemical in bones makes them stiff. The vinegar slowly removes this chemical from the bones. When the chemical is removed, the bones are floppy.

OTHER THINGS TO TRY:

Try other kinds of bones to see if you can make them floppy as well.

DISCOVERY
You can make a bone that will easily bend, as if it were made of rubber.

The Shrinking Cup

#6

TIME REQUIRED
about 5 minutes

What you need

✔ Styrofoam cup

✔ fingernail polish remover (containing acetone)

✔ cookie sheet, small pan, or metal or glass bowl

DO NOT USE A PLASTIC BOWL OR TRAY FOR THIS EXPERIMENT.

WHAT TO DO

1. Place the cup in the pan.

2. Fill the cup about half full with nail polish remover.

3. Observe what happens to the cup.

4. Pick up the melted cup and roll it into a ball or some other shape.

5. Run water down the sink and with the water running, pour the nail polish remover down the sink. Do not get the remover near your eyes or mouth.

6. When you are finished handling the melted cup, wash your hands thoroughly.

WHAT'S HAPPENING AND WHY:

 The chemical acetone in the nail polish remover destroyed the structure of the Styrofoam by removing the air that is in Styrofoam. The styrofoam shrank. If nothing happened to the cup in your experiment, try another brand of nail polish remover. Some brands do not have much acetone in them.

The ball of Styrofoam will dry and harden. Some companies now recycle styrofoam in this manner and use the hardened form to make benches or picnic tables.

You probably noticed that your hand felt cool when you removed it from the nail polish remover. When liquid evaporates from the skin, heat is removed in the process. The acetone evaporates more quickly than water, removing much heat from your hand.

OTHER THINGS TO TRY:

You can do a similar thing with Styrofoam packing materials. Place the material in a metal or glass bowl or huge glass jar. Pour some nail polish remover into the bowl. You will be amazed at how many packing pellets you can make disappear!

Homemade Slime

#7

TIME REQUIRED
10-20 minutes

WHAT TO DO

1. Dissolve 1 1/2 teaspoons of borate in 1/2 cup (100 mL) of water. The solution will appear cloudy.

2. Pour this mixture into the jar. Label the jar BORAX.

3. Measure about 1 ounce of glue (30 mL) and pour this amount into the Styrofoam cup.

4. Add 1 ounce (30 mL) of water to this cup and stir with the wooden stick.

5. Add a few drops of food coloring to the cup and keep stirring until the liquid is one color.

6. Add 1 ounce (30 mL) of the Borax solution (from step 2) to the glue-and-water mixture in the cup. Stir with a wooden stick. What happens to the mix as you stir?

What you need

✔ Styrofoam cup

✔ wooden stick or tongue depressor or chop stick

✔ white school glue (such as Elmer's)

✔ measuring cup

✔ water from faucet

✔ Borate (available in some stores as borax or Boraxo soap)

✔ teaspoon

✔ sealable plastic bag

✔ food coloring

✔ jar with lid

7. Continue to stir until almost no liquid remains.

8. Hold the cup over the sink, and remove the slimy goo from the cup. Pass the glob back and forth between your hands a few times.

9. Now do one of the following: a) let the goo run from hand to hand like slime. b) roll the goo into a ball and place it on the table.

WHAT'S HAPPENING AND WHY:

The glue contains long stringy molecules that all get hooked together by the borate. The slime behaves both like a liquid and a solid!

OTHER THINGS TO TRY:

You can keep your slime for a long time if you place it in a sealable plastic bag. If the slime starts to get flaky, moisten your hands before taking the slime out of the bag. DO NOT PUT THE SLIME IN YOUR POCKET. **ALWAYS KEEP THE SLIME IN ITS BAG WHEN YOU ARE NOT USING IT.** Try adding different colors to the slime.

Unit 2
COLOR

Imagine a world without color. It would seem very dull. Some companies have large groups of scientists who do nothing but study color.

Many colors or dyes for clothing come from plants. Some of these dyes will change colors when they are mixed with other chemicals. Other chemicals will lose their color when mixed with different chemicals.

KEY WORDS
acid
base
chromatography
solubility

#8

Changing Colors

What you need

✔ saucepan

✔ water from faucet

✔ blender or food processor

✔ red or purple cabbage leaves (NOT green cabbage)

✔ baking soda

✔ vinegar

✔ lemon juice

✔ ammonia household cleaner

✔ other household liquids such as tea, coffee, soft drinks

✔ many small jars or glasses

✔ teaspoon

✔ blueberries, radish, index card (optional)

 TIME REQUIRED
at least 10-20 minutes

WHAT TO DO

1. Have an adult boil some purple cabbage leaves in water for about 10 minutes, or have them blend some leaves with water in a blender. In either case, you should end up with a purple liquid.

2. After the purple liquid cools, put about an ounce (30 mL) in a glass or jar.

3. Add a teaspoon of vinegar to the liquid. What color is it now?

4. Repeat step 2 with a new jar, and add a pinch of baking soda to the jar. What color is the jar now?

5. Try adding other household items, such as ammonia cleaner, to a new jar of cabbage water. What color do you see now?

6. After the liquid has changed color, try to make it return to its original color.

DISCOVERY

Watch a liquid change from red to blue and back to red and then to green.

WHAT'S HAPPENING AND WHY:

Cabbage contains a chemical that changes color in the presence of acids or bases. Acids make the chemical become pink, and bases make it become purple or even dark green. Is vinegar an acid or a base?

OTHER THINGS TO TRY:

Try many different household items. If you use dark-colored liquids, such as colas, use just a small amount. Try to make layers of different colors in the same jar.

The same chemical in red cabbage is also found in blueberry juice and in radishes. Try crushing a few blueberries, adding a little water to the juice, and then adding some of the above chemicals. Crush part of a radish on an index card, and then add a drop or two of some liquid. What happens?

9

More Color Changes

TIME REQUIRED
20 minutes

What you need

✔ tumeric

✔ rubbing alcohol

✔ 2-3 small jars or glasses

✔ baking soda

✔ vinegar

✔ ammonia cleaner

✔ teaspoon

✔ measuring cup

WHAT TO DO

1. Put about 1/4 teaspoon of tumeric in a small jar.

2. Add about 1/2 cup (100 mL) rubbing alcohol. Stir with a spoon. The mixture will turn yellow-gold but many particles will still be present.

3. Pour a small amount of this liquid into 2 or 3 jars.

4. Add a small amount of vinegar to one jar; a small amount of baking soda to another; and a small amount of ammonia-based household cleaner to the last.

5. Observe the color that appears in each jar.

WHAT'S HAPPENING AND WHY:

The color in the tumeric is removed with the alcohol. The chemical that makes this color changes as the liquid becomes more basic. Baking soda made the mix slightly basic, and the ammonia made it very basic.

OTHER THINGS TO TRY:

Try other liquids and other foods to see what colors they produce. Try mixing the jars you made in this experiment. Mix some of the colors you made in the previous experiment.

Magical Voices

What you need

✔ jar with lid
✔ baking soda
✔ phenol red (available in pool stores)
✔ water from faucet
✔ straw (optional)

TIME REQUIRED
10-15 minutes

WHAT TO DO

1. Fill the jar about half full with water.

2. Add 2-3 drops of phenol red to the jar of water. Swirl the jar.

3. If the color of the liquid is not red, add 1-2 small pinches of baking soda.

4. Blow into the jar, or blow through the straw into the jar.

5. Observe what happens to the color.

WHAT'S HAPPENING AND WHY:

 Phenol red is a dye that changes from red to yellow when the solution goes from basic to acidic. When you blow, you release carbon dioxide, and this gas combines with water to make it acidic. To do the experiment again, add 1-2 pinches of baking soda until a light red color appears.

OTHER THINGS TO TRY:

Instead of using a straw, have lots of people talk into the jar. Cover the jar and swirl after each person talks. You can also use phenol red to make many different colors. Try adding some vinegar, lemon juice, or ammonia cleaner.

#11 COLORING EGGS

What you need
✔ many eggs
✔ vinegar
✔ teaspoon
✔ pan of water
✔ natural food dyes (see below)

TIME REQUIRED

30 minutes to 3 hours, depending on the food

WHAT TO DO

Have an adult simmer the eggs in boiling water and one of the coloring agents. Some agents will require 1 teaspoon of vinegar. The more agent you use, or the longer you soak the egg, the darker the color will be.

DYE	AMOUNT	COLOR PRODUCED	DYE	AMOUNT	COLOR PRODUCED
FRESH OREGANO OR FRESH MINT	2-4 tsp + vinegar	beige	RED CABBAGE LEAVES	8-10 leaves + vinegar	blue to purple
INSTANT COFFEE	2 tsp	dark brown	SPINACH LEAVES	8-10 leaves	gray-gold
GOLDEN DELICIOUS APPLE PEELS	1-2 apples + vinegar	lavendar	ONION SKINS	1/2 cup + vinegar	orange
ORANGE PEELS	1 orange + vinegar	yellow	THYME	1 tsp + vinegar	orange
STRAWBERRY	juice from 4-6 berries	pink	BLUEBERRY	4-6 berries + vinegar	blue or purple
TUMERIC	1 tsp	bright yellow	POMEGRANATE	juice from 1 piece + vinegar	bright yellow

WHAT'S HAPPENING AND WHY:

Boiling water helps to pull the color out of the food. Vinegar in some cases helps the dye to stick to the eggs.

DISCOVERY You can dye eggs by using different foods in the kitchen.

OTHER THINGS TO TRY:

Try boiling the eggs first, and then just soaking them in the dye. Try adding baking soda instead of vinegar. Try other items in your kitchen, and if they work, please let me know. Try using these dyes with boiling water and cloth.

Separating Colors to Make Pictures

TIME REQUIRED
15-30 minutes

WHAT TO DO

1. Place about 1/4 inch (5-6 mm) of water in the pan.

2. Using the pens, place many different colored dots on the coffee filter. All the dots should be at least 3/4 inch (15-18 mm) from the edge of the filter.

3. Open the coffee filter and carefully place it in the water. Do not let the water cover the dots, and do not let the filter fall into the water.

4. Allow the water to move almost to the top of the paper, then remove the filter and allow it to dry.

WHAT'S HAPPENING AND WHY:

This procedure is called *paper chromatography*. Colors move up the paper at different rates because they mix unevenly with water. You may have been surprised at what colors were in some of the original colors. Scientists use a similar procedure to separate different chemicals.

DISCOVERY
You will separate different colors and make a piece of art at the same time.

OTHER THINGS TO TRY:

Instead of a coffee filter, try a brown paper bag. Some will work and others will not. Try as many different colors as you can. Watch the separated colors run into a new color. Try different kinds of food colorings.

Clean a Dirty Penny

What you need
- ✔ soiled, dirty penny
- ✔ small plate
- ✔ spoon
- ✔ salt
- ✔ vinegar

TIME REQUIRED
5 minutes

WHAT TO DO

1. Place the penny on the plate.

2. Cover the penny with salt.

3. Add a half spoonful of vinegar to the salt on the penny.

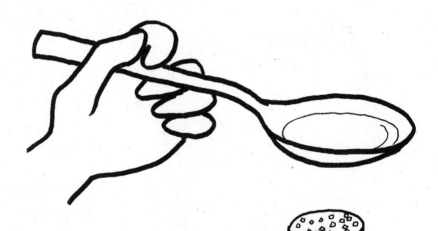

WHAT'S HAPPENING AND WHY:

The vinegar and the salt combine to form a strong acid, the same one that is produced by your stomach. Oxygen in the air combines with the copper in the penny to produce the dull color. The acid pulls the oxygen away from the copper, leaving it shiny.

DISCOVERY
A dirty penny will suddenly become shiny again.

OTHER THINGS TO TRY:

Try soaking a penny in lemon juice for 20-30 minutes instead of using salt and vinegar.

Unit 3
Water

Water is a wonderful chemical. It can take the shape of any container. It freezes, or becomes solid, at a temperature that is not too cold. It boils, or turns to gas, at a temperature that is not too hot. As water evaporates, or turns to gas, it removes much heat and makes things cooler. This is why sweating helps to keep you cool. You can add much heat to water, but the temperature will change only slowly. Many different chemicals will dissolve in water. Water molecules will stick to other water molecules.

Water is very important to life. Life as we know it would not exist without water. You could live many days without food, but you could live only 2 or 3 days without water.

KEY WORDS

control
evaporate
gas
gravity
liquid
solid
surface tension
syphon
volume

#14 Watch the Pepper Move

What you need

✔ bowl
✔ toothpick
✔ water from faucet
✔ white pepper
✔ dish detergent or liquid soap

TIME REQUIRED
10 minutes

WHAT TO DO

1. Fill the bowl with water.

2. Sprinkle pepper on the surface so that most of the surface is covered with pepper.

3. Dip the toothpick through the pepper. Does anything happen?

4. Place a drop of dish detergent on the end of the toothpick.

5. Dip the toothpick through the pepper. What happens now?

WHAT'S HAPPENING AND WHY:

Water molecules are held together in such a way that many objects will float on the surface of water. This property is called *surface tension*. The dish detergent contains molecules that are greasy, and greasy molecules don't mix well with water. The greasy molecules push in between the water molecules, and anything on the surface moves toward the side and eventually sinks.

You did a control by dipping only the toothpick first. The result showed that you must have the detergent.

OTHER THINGS TO TRY:

 Try other spices as well; some will work and others will not. If you don't have dish detergent, stick the toothpick into a bar of soap or into liquid soap.

DISCOVERY
Pepper placed on the surface of water suddenly moves toward the edge of the bowl.

#15 Floating and Sinking Needles

What you need

- ✔ small piece of tissue paper
- ✔ water from faucet
- ✔ glass
- ✔ needle
- ✔ pencil or toothpick
- ✔ dish detergent

TIME REQUIRED
10-15 minutes

WHAT TO DO:

1. Fill the glass with water.

2. Place a small piece of tissue paper on the surface of the water.

3. Carefully place the needle on the surface of the paper.

4. Slowly touch the corner of the paper with a pencil or toothpick. The paper should sink, and the needle should now be floating on the water.

5. Dip the toothpick in dish detergent and carefully touch the water with the toothpick. What happens?

WHAT'S HAPPENING AND WHY:

 Water molecules are held together in such a way as to almost have a skin. This property is called *surface tension*. The dish detergent breaks the bonds that are responsible for the surface tension, and the needle sinks. Surface tension is what allows insects to walk on water.

DISCOVERY

You can float a needle on water, and then suddenly make it sink.

OTHER THINGS TO TRY:

Try floating other objects on the surface of water. Which objects will float and which will sink?

#16

Pick Up Ice With a String

What you need

✔ salt

✔ ice cube

✔ piece of string, about 4 inches (10 cm) long

TIME REQUIRED

15-20 minutes

WHAT TO DO

1. Place the ice cube on the table.

2. Place the string on top of the ice cube. Thick string or twine works better than thin string.

3. Raise the string. Does the ice cube move?

4. Replace the string on top of the cube.

5. Sprinkle salt on top of the string.

6. Wait about 5 minutes.

7. Raise the string. Does the ice cube move now?

WHAT'S HAPPENING AND WHY:

Salt makes the ice melt and then refreeze at a lower temperature.

As the ice melts, the string forms a groove in the ice cube. As the water refreezes, it freezes around the string so that the string is now inside the ice.

OTHER THINGS TO TRY:

Try strings of different thicknesses.

Try placing another ice cube on top of the string and the salt to see if you can make two cubes that seem to be glued together.

DISCOVERY

You can pick up an ice cube by placing a string on top of it.

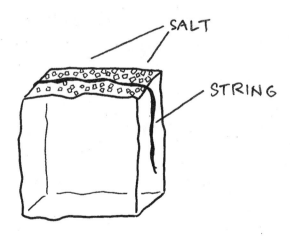

SALT

STRING

#17

Make a Siphon!

What you need

✔ 2 jars

✔ plastic rubber tubing (available in pet stores)

✔ water from faucet

THIS EXPERIMENT MUST BE DONE OVER THE SINK.

TIME REQUIRED

15 minutes

WHAT TO DO

1. Fill a jar about 3/4 full with water and place it on the counter near the edge of the sink.

2. Place the empty jar in the sink.

3. Hold the tube upside down and fill it with water from the faucet.

4. Pinch one end of the tube and place the other end in the jar with water. (Keep it pinched tight!)

5. Place the pinched end in the empty jar and unpinch the end. Watch what happens to the water.

WHAT'S HAPPENING AND WHY:

The device you have made is called a *siphon*. Gravity causes water to move from a higher to a lower place, and water molecules tend to stick to each other. As the water leaves the tube, air pushes on the water in the jar and forces more water into the tube.

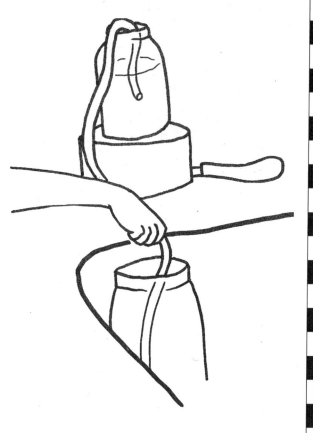

DISCOVERY
You can move water from one container to another without pouring the water.

OTHER THINGS TO TRY:

If the water does not move from the full jar to the empty jar, remove the tube and empty all the water. Place the tube in the full jar and suck water into the tube. Quickly put the tube into the empty jar. Try different heights between the empty and full jars. Can you think of any uses for siphons?

#18 The Case of the Disappearing Water

TIME REQUIRED
10-15 minutes

WHAT TO DO:

1. Tear a piece of the diaper so that it just covers the bottom of the cup.

2. Carefully pour water into the cup, making sure that you pour it onto the diaper.

3. Turn the cup upside down. No water should come out.

WHAT'S HAPPENING AND WHY:

 The chemical that is used to make most disposable diapers absorbs LOTS of water. If you do this in front of friends, don't let them see that the cup has a diaper in the bottom.

OTHER THINGS TO TRY:

 Try to determine how much water you can put on a piece of diaper before it is no longer absorbed. Compare different brands of diapers and also use different brands of paper towels. You don't have to put the diaper in a cup. You can just place it on the counter and pour water into it.

DISCOVERY

This is a great experiment to do in front of friends. When you pour water into a cup and turn the cup upside down, no water comes out of the cup.

#19 Joining Streams of Water

What you need
✔ plastic milk jug
✔ pencil
✔ water from faucet

THIS EXPERIMENT MUST BE DONE OVER THE SINK.

 TIME REQUIRED
10-15 minutes

WHAT TO DO

1. Use the pencil to poke 3 or 4 holes near the bottom of the jug. The holes should be about 1/4 inch (6 mm) apart.

2. Fill the jug half full with water and hold the jug over the sink. You should see water streaming from each hole.

3. With your thumb and first finger, slowly pinch the streams of water until your fingers touch.

4. Remove your finger. Do you see just one stream?

WHAT'S HAPPENING AND WHY:

Water molecules are attracted to other water molecules. This behavior makes water stick together. When you pinched the streams of water, the molecules from one stream were attracted to those of another stream.

DISCOVERY

Many streams of water coming from a jug can be made to form just one stream.

OTHER THINGS TO TRY:

Try making the holes closer together or farther apart. Try making different sized holes. Instead of water, try putting some cooking oil or rubbing alcohol in the jug, and see if you can make one stream.

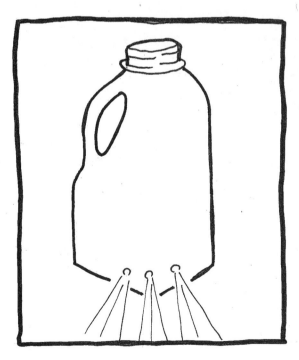

#20 How Clean Is the Air?

What you need

- ✔ water from faucet
- ✔ jar
- ✔ funnel
- ✔ coffee filter or 2 or 3 sheets of paper towel
- ✔ magnifying glass (optional)

TIME REQUIRED

5 minutes to set up; then 10 minutes 2-3 days later

WHAT TO DO

1. Fill the jar about half full with water.

2. Place the jar outside and wait 2-3 days. Make sure you don't cover the jar!

3. Place the coffee filter or paper towel sheets in the funnel.

4. Examine the water and then slowly pour the water from the jar into the funnel. <u>YOU MUST DO THIS STEP OUTSIDE.</u>

5. Examine the filter. Use a magnifying glass if you have one. Try to count the number of particles that are on the paper.

WHAT'S HAPPENING AND WHY:

The filter probably turned dark. Particles of dirt, smoke, and pollen that are in the air fell into the water. You trapped these particles on the paper. This is an experiment similar to what environmental scientists do to see how clean the air is.

OTHER THINGS TO TRY:

Collect air samples at different times of the year. Place jars in different locations to see if different places have different amounts of particles.

#21

Push the Top Off

TIME REQUIRED

 5 minutes, then 5 minutes 4-5 hours later

WHAT TO DO

1. Fill the canister to the very top with water.

2. Very carefully put the lid on the canister. Be sure not to spill any water.

3. Put the canister in the freezer. Make sure nothing is on top of the canister.

4. Wait 4-5 hours then look at the canister.

WHAT'S HAPPENING AND WHY:

 Most things get smaller as they cool and freeze, but water is different. It actually expands as it freezes. The water molecules tend to form rings as they freeze, and the rings take up more room than if they were not hooked together. The cap came off because the water molecules took up more room as they froze.

A similar thing happens to water pipes in the winter. If they freeze, and then begin to thaw, the ice can actually make the pipes burst.

OTHER THINGS TO TRY:

Try putting the canister in without the top. Use other containers instead of the film canister, but just be sure each has a top. Try putting fruit juice instead of water in the canister.

Unit 4
Mass and Density

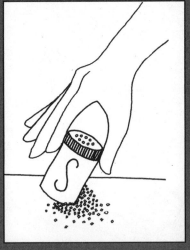

Density is a measure of how much space or volume a certain amount of mass takes up. A pound or kilogram of nails takes up less space than a pound or kilogram of feathers. Feathers are light, or have a low density. Solids will float on top of liquids if the density of the solid is less than the density of the liquid.

Some liquids will mix easily with water, and when these two liquids mix, the mix will look the same throughout. Other liquids will not mix well with water. In this case, two distinct layers are formed.

In order for an object to be balanced on top of another object, the mass must be distributed evenly around a point. Some of the experiments in this section involve the distribution of mass.

KEY WORDS
balance
corrugated
cylinder
density
displace

#22 A Floating Egg

What you need

- ✔ glass
- ✔ uncooked egg
- ✔ salt
- ✔ water from faucet
- ✔ spoon

TIME REQUIRED
10 minutes

WHAT TO DO

1. Fill the glass half full with water.

2. Place the egg on the spoon and carefully place the egg in the water. What happens to the egg?

3. Remove the egg from the glass. Place it on the counter.

4. Add 7-10 spoonfuls of salt to the water in the glass. Stir until it all dissolves. The water will seem a little cloudy.

5. Use the spoon to carefully place the egg in the water. What happens to the egg?

WHAT'S HAPPENING AND WHY:

The egg sank because it had a larger, or higher, density than the water. When you put the salt in water, you increased the density of the water so it was in fact higher than the density of the egg. The egg now floats.

It is easier to float in the ocean than in a pool or lake because salt water is denser than regular water. The Great Salt Lake in Utah has so much salt that it is almost impossible to sink.

OTHER THINGS TO TRY:

Try different amounts of salt in water to determine the minimum amount necessary to float the egg. For a great magic trick in front of people, try this: Dissolve many spoonfuls of salt in some water. Slowly pour this salt solution into a glass of water that has an egg at the bottom. At some point, the egg will begin to rise and float.

The Case of Sinking Ice

#23

What you need
- ✔ ice cubes in a bowl
- ✔ 2 glasses about the same size
- ✔ water from faucet
- ✔ rubbing alcohol

TIME REQUIRED
10-15 minutes

WHAT TO DO

1. Fill one glass with water and one glass with rubbing alcohol.

2. First place an ice cube in a glass of water. Does it float or sink?

3. Now place another ice cube in the glass of alcohol. Does this cube float?

WHAT'S HAPPENING AND WHY:

Alcohol has a lower density than the density of water or ice. When you place the ice cube in the alcohol, it quickly sinks to the bottom. Because alcohol is less dense than water, alcohol will actually float on top of water (see Experiment 24).

OTHER THINGS TO TRY:

👉 Try mixing equal amounts of alcohol and water and see if the ice floats or sinks. For a more striking demonstration, prepare some large, colored ice cubes by mixing food coloring with water before freezing.

#24

How Many Layers Can You Make?

What you need

- ✔ clear, tall glass or jar
- ✔ water from faucet
- ✔ cooking oil
- ✔ mineral oil
- ✔ rubbing alcohol
- ✔ concentrated dish detergent
- ✔ honey or syrup
- ✔ food colorings (optional)

TIME REQUIRED

20-30 minutes

WHAT TO DO

1. Pour some honey or syrup into the glass.

2. Slowly pour some dish detergent down the inside of the glass.

3. Slowly pour some water on top of the detergent.

4. Pour some mineral oil or cooking oil down the inside of the glass.

5. Pour some rubbing alcohol down the inside of the glass.

6. Observe the glass. You should see many different layers.

WHAT'S HAPPENING AND WHY:

 All of the liquids have different densities. The liquids with lighter

54

densities will float on top of those liquids with heavier densities. Some of the layers will eventually mix with other layers because one of the chemicals will dissolve in the other. Other layers will remain forever because some of the liquids do not mix.

DISCOVERY
Make as many layers as possible in a glass.

OTHER THINGS TO TRY:

To make it easier to see some of the layers, try putting different food colorings in different liquids. This step will produce many different layers of different colors. Try adding the lighter liquids first, then add some of the denser liquids to see if you still get layers. Try other liquids that you may find in the kitchen and try to make as many layers as possible. I have made 13 layers with liquids I found in the kitchen and bathroom.

After you have made the layers, slowly drop a coin, a grape, a piece of rice, a piece of pasta, a cork, and then a piece of styrofoam into the glass. Observe where each object ends up.

#25 Can You Balance Many Nails?

What you need

✔ piece of wood at least 1 1/2 inches (4 cm) thick

✔ hammer

✔ 12-14 nails at least 4 inches (10 cm) long

TIME REQUIRED
10-15 minutes

WHAT TO DO

1. Have an adult pound one nail into the board. The nail must be straight and must not come through the other side of the wood.

2. Lay one nail on the table. Place the other nails on top of this nail with the ends going in opposite directions (see drawing).

4. Place the last nail on top of the first nail, but put it in the opposite direction of the first nail.

5. Pick up all the nails and carefully place them on the nail that is in the wood. All the nails should now be balanced.

WHAT'S HAPPENING AND WHY:

To balance objects, you must distribute the mass evenly around a point. The structure you made distributes the mass evenly on each side of the nail. The top nail is used to hold all the other nails together.

OTHER THINGS TO TRY:

Try more than 12 nails. Try nails of different sizes.

DISCOVERY

Challenge a friend to balance 10-12 nails on one other nail. He or she will probably be unable to do it, but you will!

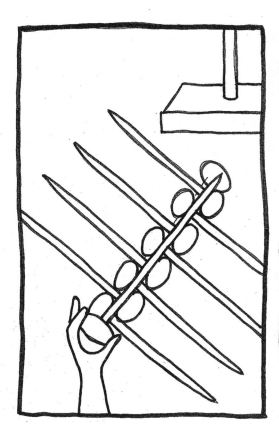

#26 Leaning Salt Shaker

What you need
- ✔ table or counter top
- ✔ salt shaker (a glass one works best)
- ✔ lots of salt

 TIME REQUIRED
10 minutes

WHAT TO DO

1. Make a pile of salt on the table.

2. Place the salt shaker in the pile, and move it around until it is balanced on its side. This may take some practice.

3. Carefully remove and blow away the excess salt so the table now appears clean.

4. Carefully walk away and leave the leaning salt shaker.

WHAT'S HAPPENING AND WHY:

When you balanced the shaker in the pile of salt, grains of salt were on different edges of the salt shaker. These grains were all pushing on the shaker and keeping it balanced. You removed the excess salt, but the support grains remained in place. Most people cannot see them, and the shaker looks like it is mysteriously leaning in the air. Shakers that have straight edges will work better than shakers that have rounded edges. Be sure to clean up all the salt that you poured initially.

DISCOVERY
Balance a salt shaker on its side.

OTHER THINGS TO TRY:

This principle can be used to balance many other small objects in a tilted position. Try it with some small toys.

Unit 5
Motion

Why do objects move? A force (a push or pull) is applied to an object. This force can come from many different sources such as air, gravity, machines, heat, etc. As an object moves, it usually will slow down because of *friction*. Friction occurs when two or more objects rub against each other.

A very important rule of motion is the *Law of Inertia*. This law, first proposed by Isaac Newton, says that an object in motion will tend to stay in motion, and that an object at rest will tend to stay at rest, unless a force is applied to the object.

As you do the experiments in this section, try to figure out what kind of force is acting, and whether the force is pushing or pulling.

KEY WORDS

compress

energy

force

friction

gravity

inertia

pendulum

#27 Replace the Bottom Penny

What you need

✔ 10-15 pennies (or any identical coins)

⏰ TIME REQUIRED
10 minutes

WHAT TO DO

1. Make a stack of 5 pennies.

2. Place another penny on the table, about 2 inches (5 cm) away.

3. Use your finger to flick the penny so that it hits the stack. You may have to try this motion a few times.

4. Observe what happens to the penny at the bottom of the stack when hit.

WHAT'S HAPPENING AND WHY:

 This is one of many experiments that deals with the law of inertia. The stack of pennies was at rest. The energy of the moving penny was transferred to the stack and the bottom penny began to move.

DISCOVERY
Move the bottom penny
from a stack of pennies
without touching it with
your hand.

OTHER THINGS TO TRY:

Try making different height stacks.
Use a different coin as the moving
object. Try moving the penny from different distances. Can you figure out how to
move more than one penny?

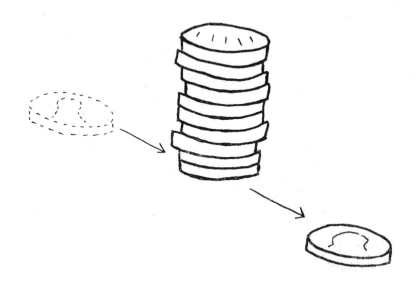

Put a Coin in a Jar

What you need

- ✔ glass or jar
- ✔ index card
- ✔ coin
- ✔ pencil

TIME REQUIRED
10 minutes

WHAT TO DO

1. Place the index card on top of the jar.

2. Place the coin in the middle of the card.

3. Quickly tap the pencil against the edge of the card. The card must move horizontally. It may take some practice to hit the card so that it will move horizontally and the penny will fall.

WHAT'S HAPPENING AND WHY:

 The coin was at rest, and tended to stay at rest. When you hit the card, the card moved, but the energy was not transferred to the coin. The coin did not move horizontally. It did fall because gravity was pulling it down, and the card no longer held it up.

The law of inertia applies when you are in an automobile that suddenly stops. You are moving and tend to keep moving through the windshield. The seatbelt exerts a force against you and keeps you from moving. Always wear your seatbelt!

OTHER THINGS TO TRY:

Put many coins on the card and see if you can get them all into the glass. Bend your elbow and place a coin on your elbow with the open part of your hand pointing up. As you straighten your arm, move your hand and try to catch the falling coin. See the next experiment for a similar, but more striking use of inertia.

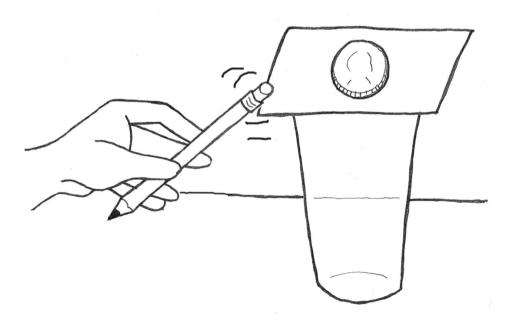

Put a Pencil in a Jar

TIME REQUIRED
10-20 minutes

WHAT TO DO

1. Place the roll of tape on top of the bottle.

2. Carefully balance the pencil on top of the tape so that the pencil is directly over the opening of the bottle.

3. Place your thumb and index finger inside the roll of tape.

4. Quickly flick your finger horizontally against the inside of the roll of tape. This last step will probably require some practice. The roll must be hit correctly and move horizontally in order for the pencil to fall into the jar. An adult may have more luck hitting the tape.

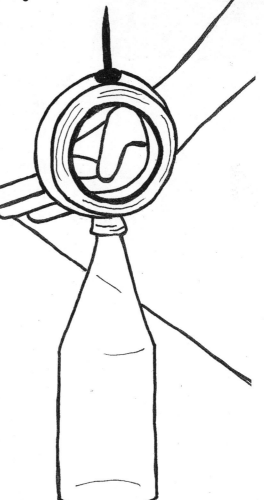

DISCOVERY

A pencil balanced on top of a ring suddenly falls directly into a jar.

WHAT'S HAPPENING AND WHY:

Another example, and probably more dramatic, of inertia. When you hit the roll, there was nothing to support the pencil, and it fell into the bottle.

OTHER THINGS TO TRY:

Try balancing two short objects on top of each other and then try to put both of them into the jar.

Launch the Ball

What you need
✓ 2 balls of different sizes

TIME REQUIRED
10-15 minutes

WHAT TO DO

1. Hold the large ball in one hand. Place the smaller ball on top of the larger ball with the other hand.

2. Remove both hands at the same time. It may take some practice to be able to drop both balls at the same time.

3. Observe what happens to the small ball.

WHAT'S HAPPENING AND WHY:

Both balls fall at the same rate. When the larger ball hits the ground, the air in this ball compresses, or gets smaller and then expands, or gets larger. As the air in the larger ball gets larger, it pushes on the wall of the large ball and also on the small ball. The force from the larger ball causes the smaller ball to fly high into the air.

OTHER THINGS TO TRY:

Put the small ball in different positions on top of the larger ball. Different positions will launch the small ball in different directions. Try dropping three balls, each of different size. Try dropping two balls of the same size.

#31 Don't Spill the Water!

What you need
✔ water from faucet
✔ bucket with handle

THIS EXPERIMENT MUST BE DONE OUTSIDE.

TIME REQUIRED
5-10 minutes

WHAT TO DO

1. Fill the bucket with water.

2. Quickly spin the bucket in a circle like a windmill. What happens to the water?

WHAT'S HAPPENING AND WHY:

Normally, if you turn a bucket upside down, water will come out because gravity is pulling on the water. When you spin a bucket in a circle, a force pushes the water to the outside of the circle. When the bucket is over your head and moving, the force is stronger than the force of gravity. Water stays in the bucket.

OTHER THINGS TO TRY:

Determine how fast you must spin the bucket to keep the water in it. Try swinging the bucket in a circle sideways rather than over your head.

#32 Don't Get Hit With the Ball

What you need
- ✔ tape
- ✔ rubber ball such as a tennis ball
- ✔ string at least 6 feet (2 meters) long
- ✔ something to hook the string to, such as a branch

 TIME REQUIRED
10-15 minutes

WHAT TO DO

1. Tape the end of the string to the ball. Be sure it is firmly attached to the ball.

2. Tie the other end of the string to a branch or hook.

3. Adjust the string so that it hangs to the height of your nose.

4. Holding the ball, take 1-2 steps backward so the ball and string are no longer straight down.

5. Hold the ball next to your nose and let go. DO NOT PUSH THE BALL!

6. Stand still as the ball returns toward your nose. (Don't worry; it will not hit you.)

WHAT'S HAPPENING AND WHY:

An object that swings back and forth is called a *pendulum*. As a pendulum swings, it never returns to its starting point unless it is pushed or pulled by some force. The air around the pendulum pushes on it and slows it down.

A playground swing is an example of a pendulum. Unless you move your body, it will never go as high as the first height.

DISCOVERY

If you hold a ball on a string near your nose and let go, you will not get hit with the ball.

OTHER THINGS TO TRY:

Find as many different examples of pendulums as you can. Determine how long it takes the pendulum to make one full swing on each trip.

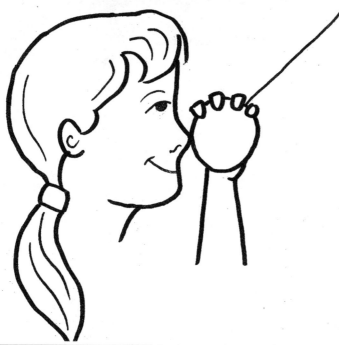

Unit 6
Properties of Air

Air is all around us. Air pushes on objects and can cause them to change shape or move. Air expands when it is heated, and contracts when it is cooled. Air moves well around curved surfaces, but poorly around flat surfaces.

Air is a gas. In a gas, molecules are far apart from each other. Gases can fill any space, such as a twisted balloon. The air that we breath is made up mostly of the gases oxygen and nitrogen.

KEY WORDS

Bernoulli's principle

expand

force

friction

pressure

sublimation

vacuum

#33 Water Rocket

What you need

- ✔ cardboard or wood at least 12 inches (30 cm) on each side
- ✔ rocks or books to make a ramp
- ✔ two-liter soft plastic soft-drink bottle
- ✔ tire stem valve (available in auto supply store)
- ✔ hand operated bicycle tire pump
- ✔ measuring cup
- ✔ water (at least 2 quarts or 2 liters)
- ✔ funnel (optional)

THIS EXPERIMENT MUST BE DONE IN AN OPEN FIELD.

TIME REQUIRED

 about 30 minutes to set up; after that about 5 minutes per flight

WHAT TO DO

1. To make the launching pad, place the wood or cardboard on some rocks or books so that you have a ramp. Wood will make a longer lasting launching pad, but cardboard will also work.

2. Put on your safety goggles.

3. Place the tire valve into the mouth of the soft-drink bottle.

4. Place the bottle on the ramp. The valve should be near the end of the ramp.

5. Attach the valve from the pump to the valve of the bottle. BE SURE TO POINT THE BOTTLE AWAY FROM YOU.

6. Start pumping air into the bottle. After a few pumps the rocket will launch.

WHAT'S HAPPENING AND WHY:

 This experiment deals with one of Newton's Laws of Motion: for every force, there is an equal force in the opposite direction. As you pumped air into the bottle, the pressure inside the bottle increased. Eventually the pressure was so much that it pushed the valve out of the bottle. This force caused an opposite force to push the bottle upward.

OTHER THINGS TO TRY:

1. Try putting different amounts of water in the bottle before pumping.

2. Try building a launching pad so that the bottle is upright.

3. Figure out what is the best size for the rocket by cutting off the bottom of another bottle and making your rocket longer.

4. Put fins of plastic on the rocket to help it go straighter.

#34

How Did the Egg Get Into the Jar?

What you need

- ✔ 1 egg
- ✔ jar (the mouth of the jar should be slightly smaller than the egg)
- ✔ saucepan
- ✔ water from faucet
- ✔ stove
- ✔ straw (optional)

 TIME REQUIRED
about 15 minutes

WHAT TO DO

1. Have an adult prepare a hard-boiled egg by heating the water on the stove. Allow the egg to cool.

2. Remove the shell from the egg.

3. Turn on the hot water faucet and let it run until it gets hot.

4. Fill the jar with hot water and let the water sit in the jar for about 3 minutes.

5. Pour out the water.

6. Place the egg on top of the jar.

7. Watch the egg. It will suddenly get sucked into the jar.

WHAT'S HAPPENING AND WHY:

Hot air takes up more space than cool air. When you put the egg on the jar, the air inside the jar was hot. As the air inside the jar cooled, the air outside pushed on the egg more than the air on the inside of the jar. The air outside forced the egg into the jar.

OTHER THINGS TO TRY:

To get the egg out of the jar, turn the jar upside down and blow into the jar with a straw. BE CAREFUL! The egg may quickly be forced out and hit you on the head. If this procedure does not work, you will have to break the egg into many pieces.

DISCOVERY

Imagine watching an egg suddenly move into a jar.

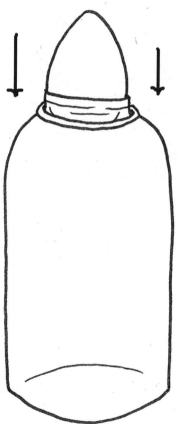

#35 Stop That Leaky Bottle

TIME REQUIRED

10-15 minutes

What you need

✔ empty plastic soft-drink bottle with lid

✔ scissors or knife (for the adult to use)

✔ water from faucet

THIS EXPERIMENT MUST BE DONE OVER A SINK.

WHAT TO DO

1. Have the adult make a small hole in the soft-drink bottle about 2 inches (5 cm) from the bottom.

2. Turn the bottle on its side so the hole is facing up.

3. Pour water into the top of the bottle until the bottle is about 1/2–3/4 full with water.

4. Hold the bottle over the sink and straighten the bottle. What happens to the water in the bottle?

5. Quickly put the lid on the bottle. What happens to the water now?

6. Slowly open the lid and observe what happens to the water.

WHAT'S HAPPENING AND WHY:

When a bottle empties, air replaces the water in the bottle. With the lid off, air can enter the bottle from the top, and water can leave from the bottom. With the lid on, the only place for air to enter the bottle is through the same opening the water is trying to leave. The air pushes on the water and keeps it from leaving the bottle.

Water jugs make use of this principle. Most of them have a spout for the water and also some small hole near the top. See if you can find the hole.

OTHER THINGS TO TRY:

Imagine you have a huge water jug that does not want to drain. You can't find a hole on the top. What can you do to get some water out?

DISCOVERY

You have come upon a soft drink bottle that is leaking because it has a hole in it. You can stop the leak without patching the hole.

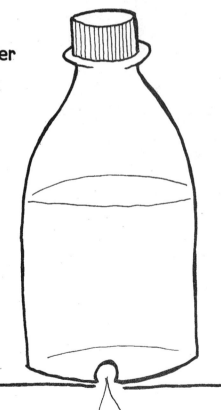

Breaking a Stick With Newspaper

 TIME REQUIRED
10-15 minutes

What you need

✔ slat of wood, 1/8 to 1/4 inch (2-5 mm) thick, 1-2 inches (2-5 cm) wide and 18-24 inches (50-75 cm) long

✔ 2-3 sheets of newspaper

WHAT TO DO

1. Place the wood on a table so that about 6 inches (15 cm) hangs over the edge.

2. Hit the wood hard with your fist. The wood should rise off the table. (Don't let it hit you in the face!)

3. Return the wood to the table.

4. Open a sheet of newspaper, place it over the wood, and smooth out the paper with your hands. The edge of the paper should touch the end of the table.

5. Place 1 or 2 more sheets of newspaper on top of the first. Be sure to smooth the sheets as much as possible.

6. Hit the wood with your fist just as you did in step 2. What happens this time?

WHAT'S HAPPENING AND WHY:

Air pushes on all objects. Without the newspaper, the air is pushing down only on the wood. When you cover the wood with paper, the air then pushes down on all the area of the newspaper. Smoothing out the paper removes any air from underneath it. The amount of air now pushing on the newspaper is about the same as having a car sitting on the wood!

DISCOVERY

You can cover a flat piece of wood with a newspaper and then break the board. Most people think the paper will fly into the air.

OTHER THINGS TO TRY:

This experiment will also work with a tongue depressor and a sheet or two of notebook paper. Try different thicknesses of wood. Try pieces of wood with different areas.

#37 The "Magic" Bottle

What you need

✔ small narrow-mouthed bottle

✔ balloon

✔ pan of cold water

✔ pan of hot water

TIME REQUIRED
5-10 minutes

WHAT TO DO

1. Place the end of the balloon over the mouth of the bottle. Make sure the balloon is secure.

2. Place the jar with the balloon in a pan of cold water for 5 minutes.

3. Now place the balloon in a pan of hot water for 5 minutes. Watch what happens to the balloon.

4. Now return the bottle to the cold water. What happens to the balloon now?

WHAT'S HAPPENING AND WHY:

 Air expands or takes up more space as it gets warmer. Placing the bottle in the hot water heated the air in the bottle. The only place the expanding air can go is into the balloon. Placing the balloon in cold water causes the air in the bottle to take up less space, and the balloon shrinks.

OTHER THINGS TO TRY:

You can use the above idea to make non-bouncy tennis balls bounce again. Wrap the balls in aluminum foil and have an adult place them in a 200° F (93°C) oven for 10-15 minutes. The balls will now bounce more because the air has expanded.

Blow up a balloon and measure its diameter. Place the balloon in the refrigerator for 15-30 minutes and measure the diameter again. See the next experiment for a similar demonstration.

DISCOVERY

You can act like a magician in this experiment. A balloon will inflate or deflate depending on where you place it.

#38 A Collapsing Container

TIME REQUIRED
15-30 minutes

WHAT YOU NEED
✔ plastic milk jug with lid
✔ hot and cold water from faucet

WHAT TO DO

1. Rinse the milk jug about 10 times with cool water.

2. Turn on the hot water and let it run until it gets very hot. (Be careful!)

3. Have an adult fill the jug part-way full with hot water. Let the jug sit for 2-3 minutes.

4. Have an adult pour the hot water out of the jug.

5. Put the lid on the jug and place it on the table.

6. Watch what happens to the shape of the jug.

WHAT'S HAPPENING AND WHY:

Air expands when heated, and air pushes on all things. The hot water heated the air in the jug. As the air cooled, the air in the room pushed on the sides of the jug and it collapsed.

DISCOVERY

A container sitting on a table suddenly collapses.

OTHER THINGS TO TRY:

If the jug did not collapse, try placing it in some cool water in the sink. Or try running cold water on it. Try to reform the jug by adding hot water to it. Sometimes the jug will reform if you blow into it.

#39 Hey! Why Did the Water Move Into the Jar?

TIME REQUIRED
10 minutes

What you need

✔ short, fat candle, about 1-2 inches (2-5 cm) high and 1-2 inches (2-5 cm) in diameter

✔ plate

✔ large-mouth jar; a mayonnaise jar works well

✔ water from faucet

✔ measuring cup

✔ matches

WHAT TO DO

1. Place the plate on the counter.

2. Pour enough water onto the plate so that it is covered with water.

3. Place the unlit candle in the middle of the plate.

4. Place the jar over the candle and observe what happens to the water.

5. Remove the jar and have the adult light the candle.

6. When the candle is burning well, have the adult put the jar over the candle. What happens to the water in the dish?

7. Carefully hold the plate over the sink and remove the jar. If you do not hold the plate over the sink, you will probably have water everywhere and a mess to clean up.

DISCOVERY
Water mysteriously enters an upside-down jar.

WHAT'S HAPPENING AND WHY:

When anything burns, oxygen is used up. As the candle burns, it uses up the air (oxygen) in the jar and eventually goes out. At this point, there is less air pressure inside the jar than there is outside pushing on the water. The outside air pushes the water into the jar. Steps 4 and 6 shows that the process requires burning.

OTHER THINGS TO TRY:

Try using different-sized jars or different sized candles. Try measuring the amount of water that enters the jar under each case. Does a candle with more than one wick produce the same result? To make this experiment more exciting, place some food coloring in the water before you light the candle.

40

The Powerful Balloon

What you need
✔ round balloon
✔ 2 Styrofoam or plastic cups

 TIME REQUIRED
5-10 minutes

WHAT TO DO

1. Place the balloon over the edge of the cup so the mouth part of the balloon is on the outside of the cup.

2. Place the second cup on top of the first.

3. Hold the two cups and blow up the balloon. What happens to the cups?

4. Squeeze the end of the balloon to keep all the air inside.

WHAT'S HAPPENING AND WHY:

As the balloon expands, it pushes against the cups and removes the air. Where the balloon and cups meet, a vacuum is created, and the two cups stick to the balloon. Suction cups that hook things to the wall work in similar way.

OTHER THINGS TO TRY:

Is it possible to attach more than two cups to the balloon? You may be able to do this if you use a large balloon. If you tightly tie the end of the balloon, you can hang it and the cups up to make a mobile.

DISCOVERY
You can use a balloon to pick up many different objects.

#41

Try to Blow Out that Candle

What you need

✔ round jar or bottle
✔ candle
✔ matches
✔ book
✔ ruler (optional)
✔ funnel (optional)

 TIME REQUIRED
5-15 minutes

WHAT TO DO

1. Place the candle about 4 inches (10 cm) behind a jar.

2. Have an adult light the candle.

3. Blow at the front of the jar. You should be blowing at the same height as the flame.

4. Observe what happens to the flame. Why do you think the flame went out?

5. Now stand a book on end.

6. Place the candle a few inches behind the book.

7. Have an adult light the candle.

8. Blow at the book. What happens to the flame?

9. Have an adult move the candle so that it is beside the book.

10. Blow at the book again. Did the candle go out this time?

DISCOVERY
Imagine blowing out a candle that is behind a jar!

WHAT'S HAPPENING AND WHY:

Air travels easily around curved surfaces. When you blew at the jar, the air traveled around the jar and formed a straight path behind the jar. Air does not move well around flat surfaces, such as the book. Instead, when air hits a flat surface, it bounces off and moves sideways. Can you explain why most trucks have curved surfaces near their roofs?

OTHER THINGS TO TRY:

Try to determine how far air will travel after hitting a book and still blow out a candle. Instead of using a jar or book, try blowing at a candle through each end of a funnel. You may be surprised that you cannot always blow out the candle.

#42 Make the Soap Bubble

What you need
- ✔ bar of Ivory soap
- ✔ bars of other soaps
- ✔ microwave
- ✔ paper towels
- ✔ knife

TIME REQUIRED
10 minutes

WHAT TO DO

1. Have an adult cut off a piece of Ivory soap 1/2 inch (1 cm) to 1 inch (2.5 cm) cube.

2. Place a piece of paper towel in the microwave and place the soap on top of the paper.

3. Have an adult turn on the microwave for 10-20 seconds.

4. Have the adult remove the towel.

5. Observe the soap. Is it bubbling? If it is not, return it to the microwave and heat some more.

6. Repeat steps 1-4 with other kinds of soap.

WHAT'S HAPPENING AND WHY:

Ivory soap contains much air and also some water. When the soap was heated, the water began to heat and the air expanded. Other soaps so not have nearly the amount of air in them that Ivory does.

DISCOVERY

When a bar of soap is put into a microwave, it suddenly begins to bubble.

OTHER THINGS TO TRY:

Try lots of different soaps. Do some of them bubble if they are heated longer than the Ivory was heated?

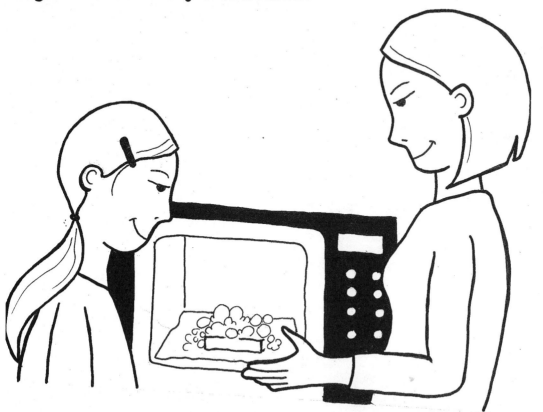

Unit 7
Sound

Sound is produced when matter moves back and forth or vibrates in the air. The vibrations cause the air to vibrate at a certain rate or *frequency*. High-frequency vibrations produce sounds that have a high pitch or tone. Sounds with low vibrations are low-pitched.

For you to be able to hear a sound, the vibrating air must travel to your eardrum and cause it to vibrate. Our eardrums can only vibrate at certain frequencies, and we can only hear certain sounds. Other animals can hear sounds that we cannot.

#43

Blow Out That Candle

What you need

✔ empty salt box

✔ candle (a short, stubby one works best)

✔ matches

TIME REQUIRED

10-15 minutes

WHAT TO DO

1. Remove the metal spout from the salt container.

2. Have an adult light the candle and place the candle on the table or counter.

3. Hold the box about 1 foot (30 cm) away from the flame and point the opening of the box toward the flame.

4. Thump the end of the box with your finger. You may have to try this a few times, or you may have to change the angle of the box. The candle should go out.

WHAT'S HAPPENING AND WHY:

The thump created a sound, but you may not have heard it. The sound caused the air in the box to move, and this moving air blew out the candle.

OTHER THINGS TO TRY:

Keep moving the box away from the candle and determine the greatest distance from which you can blow out the candle. Hang a few pieces of paper on some strings. Point the box at them and hit the end. Watch the papers move.

DISCOVERY

By using a sound to blow out a candle, you will demonstrate that sounds really are nothing more than moving air.

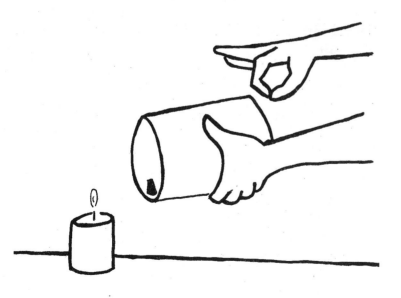

#44

Seeing the Vibrations

 TIME REQUIRED
10-15 minutes

WHAT TO DO

1. Tape the sheet of paper over the speaker by putting tape on the top edge of the paper.

2. Turn on the radio, but keep the volume low.

3. Slowly increase the volume. What happens to the paper?

4. If you have controls for *bass* and *treble*, set the bass and treble controls in the middle.

5. Turn up the volume so you can see the paper vibrate.

6. Turn the knob to full bass or full treble and observe the vibrations.

WHAT'S HAPPENING AND WHY:

The wires coming into the speaker release signals that cause a coil in the speaker to vibrate. The coil makes the speaker vibrate, which makes the air vibrate. Low-pitch sounds vibrate more slowly than do high-pitch sounds.

OTHER THINGS TO TRY:

Try to determine how many times the paper vibrates in a minute when different pitch sounds are coming through the speaker.

45

My Voice Doesn't Sound Like That

What you need
✔ tape recorder

 TIME REQUIRED
5-10 minutes

WHAT TO DO

1. Say a few words. How does your voice sound to you?

2. Turn the tape recorder to RECORD and say a few words.

3. Play back your voice. Does it sound the same as when you talk?

WHAT'S HAPPENING AND WHY:

When you hear most sounds, the sound travels down the ear canal and makes the eardrum vibrate. This vibration causes other things in your ear to vibrate, and eventually the brain records a sound. When you speak, most of the sound that you hear comes from the vibrations on the roof of your mouth. These vibrations now cause the other vibrations in your ear, but these vibrations are at a different frequency than what comes through the ear canal. The way your voice sounds on tape is the way you sound to other people.

DISCOVERY
When you listen to your voice on a tape recorder, it sounds differently than when you speak.

OTHER THINGS TO TRY:

Try speaking with a very high- or very low-pitch voice. Record these voices. Do any of the voices sound more similar to what you hear when you speak?

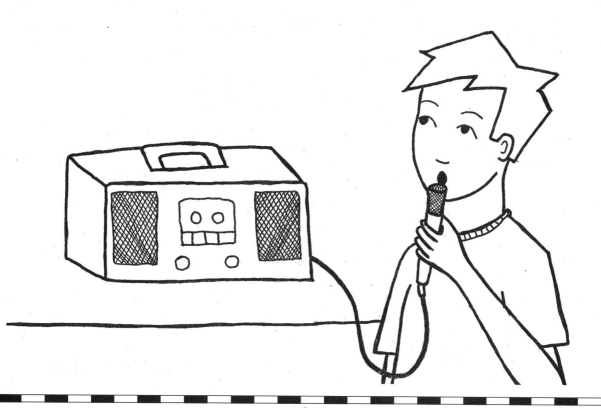

#46

SNAP Goes the Straw

 TIME REQUIRED

5-10 minutes

WHAT TO DO

1. Twist the straw so there is a bulge in the middle.

2. Hold this straw tightly and have a friend flick the straw with a finger.

3. Observe what happens.

WHAT'S HAPPENING AND WHY:

By twisting the straw, you trapped air inside the straw. When you snapped your finger against the straw, you made the air move a little and created more pressure inside the straw. This pressure forced the straw to snap; and when the air escaped, it created a sound.

OTHER THINGS TO TRY:

👉 Blow up a balloon or paper bag, and pop it. Try putting two or three knots into a straw. Use straws with different diameters.

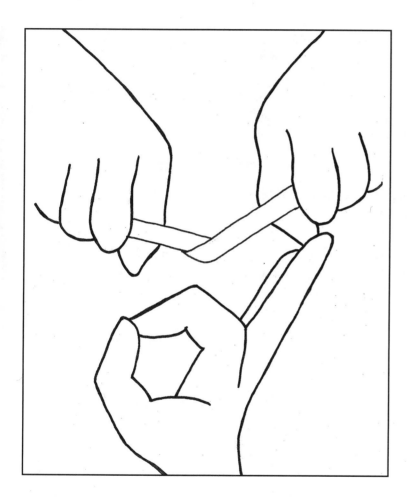

#47 Musical Coat Hanger

 TIME REQUIRED

10 minutes

WHAT TO DO

1. Tie the pieces of string to the ends of the coat hanger.

2. Loop the other ends of the strings around your opposite fingers 2 or 3 times. Do not make the loops too tight.

3. Make sure the strings stay on your fingers, and place your fingers in your ears.

4. Bend over and bang the coat hanger on the edge of the table or counter. Can you hear a sound?

WHAT'S HAPPENING AND WHY:

 When you hit the hanger, it starts to vibrate, and the vibrations travel up the string to your ear. The vibrations make your eardrum vibrate. The sound you heard probably sounded like your head was inside a bell.

OTHER THINGS TO TRY:

Try different kinds of strings or strings of different lengths. Bend the coat hanger into a square and determine if the same sound is produced. Tie the string to a spoon or other object and do the experiment. Do all the objects produce the same sound?

#48

Musical Glasses

What you need

✔ at least 4 glasses or jars, all the same size

✔ spoon

✔ water from faucet

✔ measuring cup (optional)

TIME REQUIRED

10-20 minutes

WHAT TO DO

1. Fill a glass almost full with water.

2. Tap the glass with the spoon. Is the sound high- or low-pitched?

3. Place a small amount of water in a second glass.

4. Hit this glass with the spoon. Was this sound higher or lower than the first sound?

5. Put different amounts of water in the other glasses, and tap each one with the spoon.

WHAT'S HAPPENING AND WHY:

Tapping the glass makes the glass vibrate. The water in the glass slows down the vibrations. The air above the water then vibrates more slowly. What kind of glass should have the highest pitch?

OTHER THINGS TO TRY:

Try tapping the glasses in different orders to make a song. Try different sized glasses or use plastic containers. Use a glass that has a small amount of water and tap below the water and above the water. Do you hear different sounds? See Experiment 49 for another way to make music.

49

Musical Bottles

What you need

- ✔ 4 or more bottles, all the same size
- ✔ water from faucet

TIME REQUIRED
10-20 minutes

WHAT TO DO

1. Put a small amount of water in a bottle.

2. Hold the bottle just below your bottom lip and blow cross the opening of the bottle. If you don't get a sound, move the bottle slightly and try again until you get a sound.

3. Repeat steps 1 and 2 but use bottles that have different amounts of water in them. Which bottle produces the lowest pitched sound?

WHAT'S HAPPENING AND WHY:

When you blew across the bottle, some air traveled down into the bottle. This air hit the water, and bounced up and out of the bottle. When this air left the bottle, it caused more air to move back into the bottle. The bottle then had air moving up and down, making a sound.

In the bottle with just a small amount of water, the air had to travel a long way until it hit the water. The air vibrated slowly, and a low-pitched sound was produced. Why is this result the opposite of what was observed when you tapped the bottles in Experiment 48? Think about a bassoon or oboe and a flute. Both instruments have air moving through a tube, but the air travels a shorter distance in the flute. The flute has a higher-pitched sound than the oboe or bassoon.

OTHER THINGS TO TRY:

Get many people together and have each blow across a bottle with different amounts of liquid. Try putting the same amount of water into bottles of different sizes.

Unit 8
LIGHT

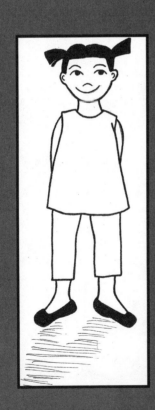

Light is another form of energy. We see things because light bounces off (*reflects*) objects and enters our eyes. Sometimes the light is reflected in such a way as to produce many images. Light travels in straight lines, but it can be bent if the surface is not flat or if light passes through different substances. The white light that we see is actually made up of many different colors of light.

KEY WORDS

concave

convex

reflect

#50 A Spoon as a Mirror

What you need

✔ shiny, metal spoon

TIME REQUIRED
5-10 minutes

WHAT TO DO

1. Hold the spoon so that the front of the spoon if facing you.

2. Look at the image of your face. Is it upside down or right side up?

3. Turn the spoon around and look into the back of the spoon. Is the image the same as it was with the spoon the other way?

WHAT'S HAPPENING AND WHY:

 The spoon acts like a curved mirror. Light is reflected off curved surfaces differently than it is off a smooth surface. When you looked at the front surface of the spoon, it behaved like a concave (curving inward) mirror, and you were upside-down. When you looked at the back of the spoon, it behaved like a convex (curving outward) mirror, and you were right-side-up. Mirrors in fun houses are not flat but curved in many ways, so the image you see is always distorted. Many telescopes use concave mirrors to focus images to a central point.

DISCOVERY
Your face will look differently depending upon which side of the spoon you look at.

OTHER THINGS TO TRY:

Try to think of different uses of convex and concave mirrors. When you see a mirror someplace, determine if it is concave or convex.

51

A Reversible Arrow

What you need

- ✔ index card or piece of paper
- ✔ pen or crayon
- ✔ clear glass or jar
- ✔ water from faucet

TIME REQUIRED
5-10 minutes

WHAT TO DO

1. Draw an arrow on the index card. The arrow should be about 2 inches (5 cm) long. Make the arrow thick.

2. Fill the glass with water.

3. Place the card behind the glass.

4. Look through the glass and slowly move the arrow away from you, then slowly bring it toward you.

5. Observe what happens to the arrow.

WHAT'S HAPPENING AND WHY:

 Light is bent by the glass and the water. When the arrow is close to the glass, the light rays from the ends cross before they reach your eyes. The arrow appears reversed from the direction it is pointing on the card. When the arrow is far from the glass, the rays do not cross, and the arrow appears as it does on the card.

OTHER THINGS TO TRY:

Try doing this experiment without water in the jar. Try using a square-shaped jar with and without water. Try putting cooking oil, mineral oil, or rubbing alcohol in the glass instead of water.

52

How Big Is Your Shadow?

What you need
✔ sidewalk chalk
✔ paper and pencil
✔ tape measure
✔ at least two people

TIME REQUIRED

5 minutes each time; the experiment should be done many times during the day

WHAT TO DO

1. Go outside and stand on the sidewalk. Use the chalk to mark where you are standing.

2. Have a friend mark where the head of your shadow is. Write down the time, both on the paper and on the shadow.

3. Wait 2 or 3 hours and return to the place where you were standing. Be sure to stand at the same spot you stood before.

4. Mark the position of the head of your shadow.

5. Repeat steps 3 and 4 two or three more times during the day. Did your shadow change position and/or size?

WHAT'S HAPPENING AND WHY:

A shadow forms because light does not pass through your body. The earth spins and moves around the sun, so the position of the sun changes throughout the day. Shadows will be shorter when the light is almost directly overhead. This is how sundials work to tell the time!

OTHER THINGS TO TRY:

Try repeating this experiment on many different days throughout the year. Instead of going outside, use a flashlight and a pencil. Move the flashlight to different places and measure the length of the shadow of the pencil.

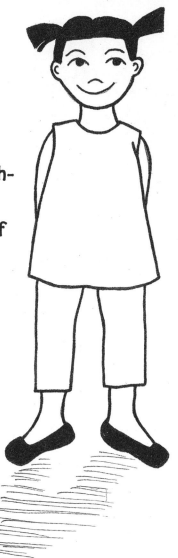

#53

I Thought Pencils Were Straight!

TIME REQUIRED
5-10 minutes

WHAT TO DO

1. Place the pencil in an empty glass. How does it appear?

2. Remove the pencil and fill the glass half full with water.

3. Place the pencil in the glass of water.

4. Look at the pencil from the side of the glass. How does it appear now?

5. Look at the pencil from above. How does it appear?

WHAT'S HAPPENING AND WHY:

As light passes through different material, it changes speed. The result is that the light is bent. When you placed the pencil in water, the light traveled at different speeds through the air and the water, and the pencil appeared bent or split.

A similar thing occurs with sound traveling through different substances. You may have heard a high, squeaky voice when someone swallowed some helium from a helium-filled balloon. Sound travels faster through helium, and thus has a higher pitch.

OTHER THINGS TO TRY:

Try making many different layers in a glass (see Experiment 24, "How Many Layers Can You Make?"). Now put the pencil in this layered glass.

How Many Pennies Do You See?

TIME REQUIRED
10-20 minutes

WHAT TO DO

1. Tape the back of the mirrors together to make one mirror that looks like a book with the reflecting side of the mirrors facing each other. The mirrors should be able to move like a hinge.

2. Open the mirrors and place the penny 1 inch (2.5 cm) away from the center of the mirrors. How many images do you see?

3. Open and close the mirrors so they form different angles, but do not move the penny. How many images do you see at each position? What is the most images you can see?

WHAT'S HAPPENING AND WHY:

An image of the penny appears in each mirror. These images are reflected onto the other mirror, forming even more images.

OTHER THINGS TO TRY:

Measure the angles between the mirrors each time you move them. Which angle gives the most images? Which angle gives the least images? Repeat the experiment but put the penny at different distances from the mirrors. Try taping three mirrors together to make a triangle. Place the penny in the middle of the mirrors. You now have made a simple kaleidoscope!

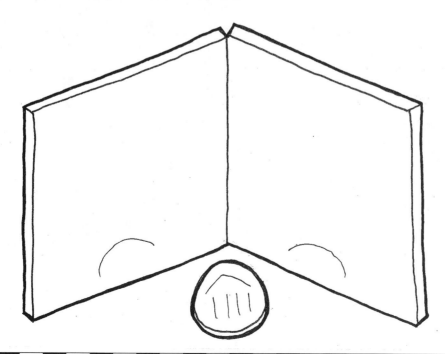

#55 Weird Color Patterns

TIME REQUIRED
20-30 minutes

WHAT TO DO

1. Place the jar on the index card and trace the jar to make a circle. Make many circles on many different cards.

2. Cut out the circles.

3. Divide the circle into three equal parts and color each part a different color.

4. Push the thumbtack through the middle of the circle and attach it to the eraser of the pencil.

5. Hold the circle in front of you and spin it between your fingers as fast as you can. What colors do you see?

WHAT'S HAPPENING AND WHY:

Our eyes usually look at one point of a moving object. As the circle spins, the colors seem to blend together. For example, as red and blue move past a point, our eye usually detects purple.

DISCOVERY
When you spin a disk with different colors, new and sometimes strange patterns appear.

OTHER THINGS TO TRY:

Try as many different combinations as you want. Try using just black lines in different places. Place different colors in different places from the center of the circle. Don't be surprised if you see some unexpected colors or some colors in some unexpected places. Scientists do not understand why certain patterns seem to change place or produce weird unexpected colors.

Unit 9
Heat, Electricity, and Magnets

From the time you were very young, you could tell the difference between hot and cold. Imagine what it must be like for people who are unable to distinguish hot from cold. Heat is a form of energy, and it always moves

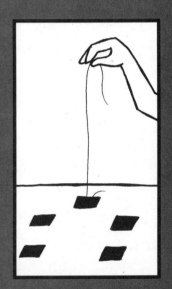

from a hot area to a colder area. Different materials gain or lose heat at different rates. Heat makes some things happen more quickly. In this unit, you will see how heat effects different events.

Electricity results from the movement of charges in a complete path or *circuit*. Some objects can be made to gain or lose one kind of charge. When this happens, some objects will have a positive charge, and others will have a negative charge. Objects with opposite charges are *attracted* to each other.

Electricity can produce magnetism, and magnetism can produce electricity. Magnets are attracted to objects that contain iron.

KEY WORDS

attract

circuit

conductor

electromagnet

expane

heat

insulator

magnetic field

repel

surface area

#56 Can You Hold a Hot Egg?

What you need

✔ egg
✔ pan of water
✔ stove or other device to cook egg

 TIME REQUIRED
30 minutes

WHAT TO DO

1. Have an adult cook the egg in the pan of water. Boil the egg for about 15 minutes.

2. Pour out the hot water and fill the pan with cold water.

3. Let the egg sit in the cold water for about 10 seconds.

4. Remove the egg and hold it in your hand for about 20 seconds. This will show your friend that the egg is cool enough to hold.

5. Give the egg to your friend and see if he or she can hold it. It will now probably be too hot to hold.

WHAT'S HAPPENING AND WHY:

Different items hold on to heat longer than others. The cold water cooled the shell but not the inside of the egg. After a while, some of the heat inside was transferred back to the shell. Heat always moves from hot areas to cooler areas.

DISCOVERY

Show a friend that you, but not she or he, can hold a cooked egg.

OTHER THINGS TO TRY:

Try soaking the cooked egg in cold water for different amounts of time before handing it to your friend. Try to determine how long it takes for the inside to be cool enough for your friend to hold it.

Time the Fizz

TIME REQUIRED
10-15 minutes

WHAT TO DO

1. Fill one glass with 1/2 cup hot water.

2. Fill another glass with 1/2 cup cold water.

3. Fill two teaspoons with baking powder.

4. At the same time, dump baking powder into each glass.

5. Observe what happens in each glass.

WHAT'S HAPPENING AND WHY:

Heat speeds up most chemical reactions. Some of the chemicals in baking powder react with water to produce carbon dioxide, the bubbles you saw. The reaction was faster in hot water. The same reaction that you observed is what happens when you drop Alka-Seltzer into water.

OTHER THINGS TO TRY:

👉 Try using different amounts of baking powder with the same temperature water.

DISCOVERY

Race a friend to see whose liquid produces bubbles faster.

BAKING SODA

#58 Stick the Balloon to the Wall

TIME REQUIRED
5-10 minutes

WHAT TO DO

1. Rub the balloon across your shirt or hair 10-20 times.

2. Place the rubbed side of the balloon on the wall.

3. Let go of the balloon. Does it stick to the wall?

WHAT'S HAPPENING AND WHY:

 Rubbing the balloon created *static electricity*. The charge on the balloon was attracted to the opposite charge of the wall. The balloon may remain attached to the wall for 5 or 10 minutes.

OTHER THINGS TO TRY:

Try to see if the balloon will stick to other objects besides the wall. Rub the balloon different numbers of times and measure how long the balloon stays on the wall for each time. For more fun with static electricity, see the next experiment.

DISCOVERY

Make a balloon stick to the wall without using any tape or hooks.

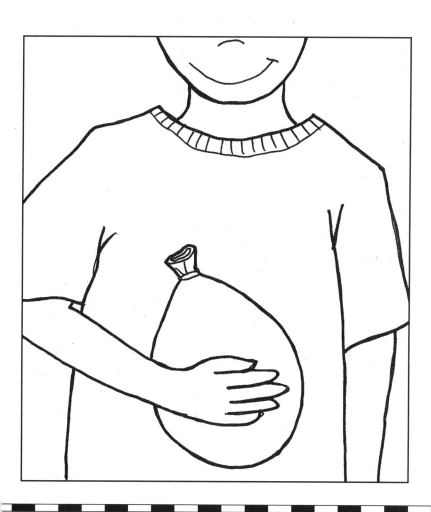

#59 Watch the Pepper Dance!

⏰ TIME REQUIRED
about 10 minutes

WHAT TO DO

1. Sprinkle some pepper onto a paper towel.

2. Rub the balloon across your shirt or hair about 15-20 times.

3. Hold the balloon a short distance above the pepper, but DO NOT TOUCH THE BALLOON TO THE PEPPER.

4. Observe what happens to the pepper.

WHAT'S HAPPENING AND WHY:

 When you rubbed the balloon, you created static electricity. Static electricity results from creating a charge on something. The charge on the balloon attracted the oppositely charged pepper, and the pepper jumped to the balloon.

DISCOVERY

Make pepper that is sitting on paper jump up into the air as if it were dancing.

OTHER THINGS TO TRY:

Try other spices to see if they will jump too. Try to determine how far the pepper will actually jump. Can you think of any uses of static electricity?

#60 Will the Magnet Make Up Its Mind?

What you need

- ✔ 5 magnets about the same size, or pieces of a magnetic strip
- ✔ string
- ✔ tape

TIME REQUIRED
10-20 minutes

WHAT TO DO

1. Form a square with four of the magnets at the corners of the square.

2. Tape the last magnet to a piece of string.

3. Hold the string so that the hanging magnet is about 1-2 inches (3-5 cm) above the other magnets.

4. Pull the magnet to one side and let it swing. Observe what happens.

WHAT'S HAPPENING AND WHY:

As the magnet moves across other magnets, it is attracted to them and then repelled by the different poles of the magnets.

OTHER THINGS TO TRY:

☞ Try to determine how far away the hanging magnet can be and still act funny. If you have small flat or round magnets, put one magnet in the middle of the square and begin turning it. Watch what happens to the other magnets.

Pick Things Up With a Nail

What you need

- ✔ battery
- ✔ nail or bolt, about 3 inches (8 cm) long
- ✔ insulated wire, about 3 feet (1 meter) long
- ✔ paperclips, thumb-tacks, etc.

TIME REQUIRED

10-20 minutes

WHAT TO DO

1. Remove the insulation from about 2 inches (5 cm) of each end of the wire.

2. Wrap the middle of the wire around the nail 40-50 times. Be sure to leave about 6 inches (15 cm) of wire at each end.

3. Touch the nail to the paperclip. Does the nail act as a magnet?

4. Hold each end of the wire to the ends of the battery, and now touch the nail to the paperclip. Does the nail now act like a magnet?

WHAT'S HAPPENING AND WHY:

 The movement of electricity creates a magnetic field. When the nail was not hooked to the battery, the nail did not behave like a magnet. Only when electricity was moving around the nail did it behave like a magnet. You created an *electromagnet*.

OTHER THINGS TO TRY:

Try the same experiment with different numbers of wraps of the wire. How many paperclips can you pick up with each different number of wraps? Try to find out about different uses of electromagnets.

Unit 10
Fun With Foods

Different types of foods are great items to use in experiments. Different foods will contain different molecules known as starches, fats, and proteins. It is simple to see which food contains fat. Remember do not eat any of the food that you use for experiments.

#62 Find That Cooked Egg!

TIME REQUIRED
30-45 minutes

What you need
- ✔ pot of water
- ✔ stove
- ✔ at least two uncooked eggs

WHAT TO DO

1. Have an adult make a hard-boiled egg for you.

2. Hold the uncooked egg upright, with the larger end on the counter or table.

3. Spin the egg and observe what happens.

4. Repeat steps 2 and 3 with the hard-boiled egg.

WHAT'S HAPPENING AND WHY:

In a hard-boiled egg, the insides have become solid and do not move around. The inside of an uncooked egg is liquid and sloshes around. When you try to spin an uncooked egg, the liquid moves, and the egg immediately falls over.

OTHER THINGS TO TRY:

👉 With the help of an adult, try to determine how long the egg has to be cooked before it will start to spin and not fall over. Cook the egg for one minute and spin; then cook the egg for another minute and spin. Continue cooking the egg extra minutes until it will spin.

DISCOVERY
Imagine that you are a food detective and that you have to tell if an egg in the refrigerator has been cooked.

#63 Find the Fat

TIME REQUIRED

 5-10 minutes to gather food; 10-20 minutes to complete

WHAT TO DO

1. Place a small piece of butter on a piece of paper.

2. Wait 2-3 minutes, then remove the butter.

3. Notice that a shiny spot appears on the paper where the butter had been.

4. Repeat steps 1 and 2 with each of the other pieces of food.

5. Make a list of all the foods that you found to contain fat.

WHAT'S HAPPENING AND WHY:

 Fat leaves a greasy, almost transparent spot on paper that is very easy to see. Many different kinds of foods have fats in them.

We hear a lot about how fat is bad for us. This statement is somewhat true. We should not eat too much fatty foods, but we must have a small amount of fat in our diet to help our cells keep the proper shape.

DISCOVERY
Try to determine which foods contain fats or grease.

OTHER THINGS TO TRY:

Test as many foods as you can for fat. You may have to ask an adult to help you put some of the foods in a blender in order to release the fat.

#64 The Great Food Detective

What you need

- ✔ talcum powder
- ✔ flour
- ✔ baking soda
- ✔ baking powder
- ✔ corn starch
- ✔ vitamin C (unflavored and crushed)
- ✔ cream of tartar
- ✔ water from faucet
- ✔ vinegar
- ✔ tincture of iodine
- ✔ 3 teaspoons
- ✔ many small pieces of paper
- ✔ pencil

TIME REQUIRED

30-60 minutes

WHAT TO DO

1. Place a small amount of baking soda on three small pieces of paper.

2. Add a spoonful of water to one pile. Observe what happens.

3. Add a spoonful of vinegar on another pile and observe what happens.

4. Add a few drops of iodine to the third pile and observe what happens.

5. Record your observations in a table similar to what appears on the next page.

6. Repeat steps 1-5 for each of the other white powders.

WHAT'S HAPPENING AND WHY:

Different chemicals are in each of the above materials, and these chemicals react differently with the three liquids you used.

DISCOVERY

You will try to determine how to distinguish different kinds of white powders.

OTHER THINGS TO TRY:

Prepare a small report describing how each chemical behaves with each liquid. Try to play real food detective by having someone prepare a mix of two or more of the powders you tested. Test it to determine what really was in the mixed powder.

HOW POWDERS REACT TO LIQUIDS

powder	water	vinegar	iodine
baking soda			
baking powder			
talcum powder			
corn starch			
flour			
cream of tartar			
vitamin C			

#65 Popping All the Popcorn Kernels

What you need

- ✔ unpopped kernels from some popcorn that has been popped
- ✔ small jar or glass
- ✔ 1/2 cup (100 mL) water
- ✔ something to pop the kernels in

TIME REQUIRED
about 20 minutes

WHAT TO DO

1. Place the "duds" or unpopped kernels in the jar.

2. Cover the kernels with water.

3. Wait about 10 minutes.

4. Remove the kernels and then have an adult help you pop them.

WHAT'S HAPPENING AND WHY:

 Popcorn pops because a little bit of water is in the kernels. As the water heats up, it turns to steam or gas. The gas, like air, pushes on the sides of the kernels until the kernels pop and the steam escapes.

Companies that say all their kernels will pop use the above idea with their popcorn. All of the kernels are usually soaked in water and then placed in tightly sealed containers. When the water evaporates or leaves the kernels, it stays in the container and is eventually pushed back into the kernels. Why do you think it is better to store popcorn in a jar than in a bag?

DISCOVERY
When you make popcorn, some of the kernels fail to pop. This experiment shows you how to get all of them to pop.

OTHER THINGS TO TRY:

Compare different brands of popcorn to see if some pop better than others. Try soaking unpopped kernels in water for different amounts of time to see if the time makes a difference in the number that pop.

#66 How Did the Balls Rise?

What you need

✔ wide-mouth jar

✔ rice

✔ 2-3 small balls: ping pong or Styrofoam ones work well

TIME REQUIRED

5-10 minutes to set up, many days for completion

WHAT TO DO

1. Place 2 or 3 balls on the bottom of a wide-mouth jar.

2. Cover the balls with rice so that the jar is at least half full with rice.

3. Place the jar on a counter or table where it will not be disturbed.

4. Look at the jar each day. At some point, the balls will be at the top of the jar.

WHAT'S HAPPENING AND WHY:

 Rice absorbs water from the air. As it does this, the pieces of rice begin to get bigger, just like they do when they are cooked. As the rice swells, it pushes on the balls and forces them to move to the top.

OTHER THINGS TO TRY:

 You can make this experiment go faster by putting 2-4 teaspoons of water on the rice each day. Try other objects instead of balls, like raisins, to see if they will also rise. Try other foods such as flour or sugar instead of rice.

DISCOVERY
When small balls are placed on the bottom of a jar of rice, they suddenly appear at the top.

#67 Dancing Food

What you need

✔ tall bottle or jar or drinking glass

✔ water from faucet

✔ baking soda

✔ vinegar

✔ teaspoon

✔ measuring cup

✔ food such as rice, raisins, or spaghetti broken into short pieces

TIME REQUIRED
10-15 minutes

WHAT TO DO:

1. Pour about 12 ounces (360 mL) of water into a tall bottle or jar.

2. Add 3 or 4 teaspoons of baking soda to the water. Stir until all the baking soda has dissolved.

3. Add a few pieces of spaghetti (about 1-2 inches or 2-5 cm long) or rice to the bottle.

4. Measure about 1 ounce (30 mL) of vinegar with the measuring cup.

5. Pour the vinegar into the bottle and gently swirl the bottle.

6. Watch what happens to the food over the next few minutes.

WHAT'S HAPPENING AND WHY:

When baking soda and vinegar are mixed, a gas called carbon dioxide is formed. The gas is lighter than the liquid and begins to rise to the surface, but as it tries to rise it attaches to the edges of the food. When enough bubbles attach to the food, it will rise to the surface. At the surface, the carbon dioxide escapes into the air, and the food sinks, waiting to bump into more gas. This process will often continue for 30 to 45 minutes. To keep the process going for a long while, swirl the bottle every few minutes.

OTHER THINGS TO TRY:

Try all sorts of food. Heavier pieces of food may require a much longer time before they rise. Try to figure out how to make the reaction go on for a long time.

DISCOVERY

Imagine looking at a bottle that contains noodles or rice bobbing up and down. You can easily make this conversation piece.

Unit 11
Biology

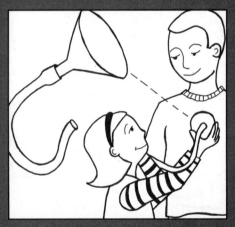

In this section you will do many different things with different kinds of plants and animals. Animals can be found almost anywhere: on the ground, under things, or in the soil, water, or air.

Most animals can move but can not make their own food. In many of the experiments, you will just be observing different kinds of animals. Do not kill any of the animals you find. All animals have an important place in the world.

Plants are almost the only form of life that can use the energy from the sun to make their own food. As plants change solar energy into chemical energy (a process known as *photosynthesis*), they give off oxygen. Most living things need oxygen to make lots of chemical energy so the cells can do many different things. Most forms of life can not exist very long without oxygen.

Many, but not all, plants start out as a seed. The seed takes in water and swells and then grows into a plant.

KEY WORDS

larvae

control

germinate

gravity

hypothesis

photosynthesis

reaction time

stethoscope

vein

#68 Watch the Ants

What you need
- ✔ bread crumbs, piece of candy, other food

TIME REQUIRED
15-30 minutes

WHAT TO DO

1. Place a piece of food outside where you can watch it. The sidewalk is a good place.

2. Look at the food every few minutes until ants appear.

3. Watch the ants patiently for the next 10 to 15 minutes. Notice how they carry food. Notice the trail they make. Do not get too close to the ants, for some of them can sting.

WHAT'S HAPPENING AND WHY:

An anthill always has a few ants out looking for food. These ants are called scouts. When the scouts find food, they go back to the hill to get more ants. The scouts leave a chemical trail for the other ants to follow, and the other ants move along this trail. Ants are very strong for their size; they can carry food that is 5-10 times heavier than they are. Pound for pound, they are stronger than people.

DISCOVERY
Watch what happens when ants discover some food.

OTHER THINGS TO TRY:

Try different kinds of food on different days to see if some foods attract ants more quickly than others. Place food in different places. You may see different kinds of ants. But don't try this inside your house—ants in the kitchen are real pests!

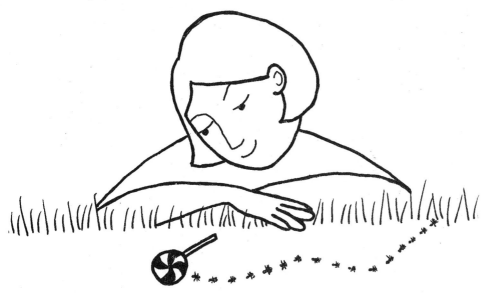

The Disappearing Blood Vessel

#69

 TIME REQUIRED
10 minutes

WHAT TO DO

1. Find one of the big veins in your arm. *Veins* are vessels that carry blood back to the heart; they usually appear bluish in the body.

2. Have your partner place a finger on one of the veins and press on this vein. (You don't need to press too hard.)

3. With the other hand, smooth out the vein by pushing toward the shoulder 2-3 times. Can you still see the vein?

4. Release the finger. What happens to the vein now?

5. Wait 2-3 minutes and then push on the same vein again.

6. This time, smooth out the vein by pushing toward the wrist 2 or 3 times. Does the vein disappear this time?

WHAT'S HAPPENING AND WHY:

Blood flows only in one direction through the body. In this case, it flows from the wrist to the shoulder. When you pressed the vein, you blocked it and prevented blood from flowing through it. You first forced the blood through the vein toward the shoulder. No new blood could enter this part of the vein. When you pushed the blood toward the wrist, blood still flowed back to the blocked area. This is a famous experiment that Sir William Harvey did over 300 years ago to show that blood moves only in one direction through the body.

OTHER THINGS TO TRY:

See if you can make another vein disappear.

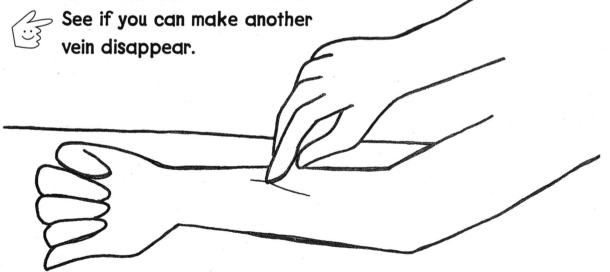

#70 Listen to Your Heart

What you need

✔ small plastic kitchen funnel

✔ plastic or rubber tubing about 18 inches (45 cm) long

 TIME REQUIRED
10-15 minutes

WHAT TO DO

1. Place the end of the tubing over the small end of the funnel.

2. Place the other end of the tubing in your ear.

3. Place the funnel over your heart (or over your partner's heart).

4. Can you hear the sound of your heart beating?

WHAT'S HAPPENING AND WHY:

The funnel serves to trap the sound produced by your beating heart. The sound then travels up the tube to your ear, just the way it does when a doctor listens to your heart. If you listen carefully, you can actually hear different sounds as the different parts of the heart beat or contract.

DISCOVERY
You can make a simple stethoscope and use it to listen to your heart.

OTHER THINGS TO TRY:

Jump up and down a few times, then listen to your heart. Does it sound the same?

#71 # Watch Your Arms Rise

What you need
✔ doorway

TIME REQUIRED
5-10 minutes

WHAT TO DO

1. Stand in a doorway with your hands at your sides. Your palms should be against your legs.

2. Lift your arms so that the tops of your wrists push against the frame of the door.

3. Push your arms against the door frame and count to 60.

4. Walk out of the door frame.

5. Take a deep breath, then exhale.

6. Observe what happens to your arms.

WHAT'S HAPPENING AND WHY:

When you walked out of the door, your muscles in your shoulders and your back were still working. All muscles do work by shortening. Your muscles continued to shorten when you left the door, and your arms continued to rise. Take some more breaths. This will help relax the muscles and bring the arms back down.

OTHER THINGS TO TRY:

Try pushing against the frame for different amounts of time. Does it make any difference if you take a deep breath when you walk out?

#72 Grab That Stick

TIME REQUIRED
10-15 minutes

WHAT TO DO

1. Grasp a meter or yard stick so that the top of your hand is at the 8 inch (20 cm) mark.

2. Open your hand and let the stick drop.

3. As quickly as possible, close your hand and catch the stick.

4. Note the number in centimeters (inches) where your hand caught the stick.

5. Subtract the starting measurement from the ending measurement.

6. Multiply this number by 4.

7. Add 90 to the number you got in step 6. Now divide this number by 1,000.

8. Write down this number. This is your reaction time in seconds.

What you need

✔ meter or yard stick

✔ paper

✔ pencil

EXAMPLE
The stick fell from 20 to 45 cm before it was caught.

45-20 = 25 (step 5)
25 x 4 = 100 (step 6)
100 + 90 = 190 (step 7)
190÷1000 = 0.190 seconds or 190 milliseconds

DISCOVERY
See how quickly you can catch a falling stick.

WHAT'S HAPPENING AND WHY:
The calculations take into account how fast something falls due to gravity. Scientists usually do an experiment more than once. Results are never exactly the same, so they often calculate an average result. You do the same thing when you calculate a test average. Note: If you use a yard stick convert all inches to centimeters by multiplying by 2.5, then perform the calculations indicated.

OTHER THINGS TO TRY:
Determine your reaction time for each arm or for different people. Try doing this experiment with one eye closed. Try to shorten your reaction time by practicing this experiment many times.

A Funny Bent Plant

TIME REQUIRED

 2-3 weeks after you have a small plant

WHAT TO DO

1. If you are using seeds, plant a few seeds in a pot as the directions on the packet indicate. Water the seeds until you have a plant that is about 3-4 inches (7-10 cm) high.

2. Once you have the plant, turn the pot on its side and place the plant where it will get the proper amount of sunlight.

3. Water the plant when the soil gets dry. To do this, you will have to turn the plant upright for a few moments. Be sure to return the pot to its side when you are done watering.

4. Observe what happens to the stem of the plant. It may take one or two weeks for the stem to bend.

WHAT'S HAPPENING AND WHY:

The top of the stem always grows up, away from the pull of gravity. This growth is the result of chemicals that are produced at the tip of the stem. When you turn the stem on its side, the stem eventually bends so that the tip grows upward.

DISCOVERY
You will make a plant with a bent, rather than a straight, stem.

OTHER THINGS TO TRY:

Once you have made the stem bend in one direction, try turning the pot so that the stem will now bend in a different direction. You can do a similar experiment by placing a plant in a position so that it gets only reflected sunlight. The plant will bend toward the direction of the sunlight. The best example of this behavior is the sunflower; these flowers turn throughout the day to follow the sun. Plants that turn toward the sun like that are called *heliotropes*.

#74 Watch the Seed Grow

What you need

METHOD 1

✔ 15-20 seeds (grass or bean seeds work well)

✔ sealable plastic bag

✔ coffee filter

✔ water from faucet

✔ spoon

METHOD 2

✔ 15-20 seeds

✔ clear plastic cup or small jar

✔ cotton

✔ water from faucet

✔ spoon

TIME REQUIRED

 5 minutes to set up; then 5 minutes each day for 1-2 weeks, depending on the seeds

WHAT TO DO

METHOD 1

1. Place the seeds on the coffee filter.

2. Add 1 spoonful of water to the filter.

3. Place the filter in the sealable bag.

4. Seal the bag.

5. Examine the bag each day for 1-2 weeks.

METHOD 2

1. Fill the cup with cotton.

2. Place the seeds along the edge of the cup, between the plastic and the cotton.

168

3. Use the spoon to moisten the cotton; do not make it too moist.

4. Examine the jar each day for 1-2 weeks. You must keep the cotton moist.

DISCOVERY
You will watch what happens when a seed is planted in the ground. This experiment can be done in one of two ways.

WHAT'S HAPPENING AND WHY:

What you see happening is what happens to seeds when they are planted. First, they begin to swell, then they begin to send out roots and stems. Notice that the root always grows down and the stem up.

OTHER THINGS TO TRY:

The first method can be used to test the effect of other solutions, such as different amounts of salt water, sugar water, tea, cola, etc. on the germination or growth of seeds.

Growing Seeds With Different Liquids

What you need

- ✔ many seeds
- ✔ 3-5 Styrofoam cups or small pots
- ✔ potting soil or dirt for all cups
- ✔ tablespoon
- ✔ water from faucet
- ✔ other liquids such as cola, orange juice, milk, tea, etc.
- ✔ paper and pencil
- ✔ ruler
- ✔ tape

TIME REQUIRED

 20-30 minutes to set up; then 10 minutes each day for 2-4 weeks

WHAT TO DO

1. Decide what kinds of seeds and what liquids you want to use.

2. Fill one cup for each liquid with dirt. Label each cup with the liquid you will use in that cup. One cup must use only water. (This is a *control*.)

3. Place 3 seeds in each cup and cover the seeds with about 1/2 inch (1 cm) of dirt.

4. Add 3 tablespoons of the appropriate liquid to the labeled cup.

5. Place the cups in a warm, sunny spot.

6. Each day, add 3 tablespoons of liquid to the cups. Do this step for 14-21 days.

7. At the end of the experiment, measure the height of the tallest plant in each group (or measure all plants and determine the average height).

8. Prepare a bar graph that shows how high the plants grew in each liquid.

DISCOVERY

Have you ever wondered whether plants would grow in liquids besides water? In this experiment you can test this hypothesis.

WHAT'S HAPPENING AND WHY:

Many of the liquids you used probably contained chemicals that plants cannot use. Plants get most of their nutrients from the soil through their roots. Some liquids contain acids or other chemicals that interfere with nutrients entering the roots. You used more than one seed because some seeds will never germinate or grow in any environment.

OTHER THINGS TO TRY:

If you got some growth with some of the liquids, try diluting the liquid with water and repeating the experiment. Try different amounts of salt or sugar dissolved in water.

Glossary

average: a number that summarizes a group of numbers

bass: low-frequency sounds

Bernoulli's principle: a rule of physics that says that moving air pushes less then non-moving air

carbon dioxide: a gas produced by mixing vinegar and baking soda; it is also produced by our bodies and exhaled

chromatography: a procedure that separates items based on colors

concave: curving inward, like a cave

conductor: a material that allows heat or electricity to move easily

control: the part of the experiment that leaves everything the way it usually is; it is used to compare a different treatment

convex: curving outward

crystal: a solid, three-dimensional shape formed from a pure chemical

density: the amount of mass in a given volume or space

electromagnet: a magnet that is produced as a result of an electric current

evaporate: to go from liquid to the vapor or gas stage

flexible: easily bent

force: a pushing or pulling on an object

frequency: the number of times an event occurs in a certain amount of time; for sound, the number of waves or vibrations per second

friction: the rubbing together of two or more objects, usually producing heat or slowing a moving object down

germinate: to start to grow

gravity: the force that is responsible for things falling toward the ground; also a large force between different planets

hydrophobic: water hating; things that are hydrophobic do not mix well with water

hypothesis: an educated guess or idea

inertia: tendency of body at rest to stay at rest or of a body in motion to stay in motion insulator: a material that prevents heat or electricity from flowing easily

mass: a measure of how much of an object is present

mineral: a natural substance made up of one type of molecule

molecule: smallest part of a compound that can exist by itself and still act like the compound

pendulum: a device on string, rope, or chain that swings back and forth but is attached at one end

photosynthesis: a process in which plants and some bacteria convert the energy in the sun to chemical energy

pitch: a measure of whether a sound is low or high; depends on the frequency of the vibrations

precipitate: to come out of solution, often by combining with something else or by changing shape

reaction time: how quickly a person responds to a signal or event

reflect: to bounce off of one object and travel to another

rigid: stiff, not easily bent

solution: mixture of dissolved materials

static electricity: a type of electricity that involves removing charges from one object.

stethoscope: a device used to listen to the beating of the heart

surface tension: a property of water that allows many objects to float on its surface

treble: sound with a high frequency

vein: a blood vessel that carries blood back to the heart

volume: how much space something takes up

About the Author

William R. Wellnitz, Ph.D., holds a B.S. and a Ph. D. from Cornell University. An associate professor of biology at Augusta State University, he began teaching children the wonders of science through ASU's Continuing Education Division. The course, known as "Wizard Wellnitz," has educated and entertained more than 1100 children over the past 10 years. More recently, Dr. Wellnitz has been the host of a weekly science show called *The Science Zone*. He is the author of four previous activity books for kids.